I'M NOT PERFECT
AND IT'S OKAY

Dolores Ayotte

I'M NOT PERFECT
AND IT'S OKAY

— A Baker's Dozen —
Thirteen Steps to a Happier Self

TATE PUBLISHING & *Enterprises*

Published by Tate Publishing & Enterprises, LLC
127 E. Trade Center Terrace | Mustang, Oklahoma 73064 USA
1.888.361.9473 | www.tatepublishing.com

Tate Publishing is committed to excellence in the publishing industry. The company reflects the philosophy established by the founders, based on Psalm 68:11,
"The Lord gave the word and great was the company of those who published it."

Book design copyright © 2008 by Tate Publishing, LLC. All rights reserved.
Cover design by Amber Lee
Interior design by Stefanie Rooney

Published in the United States of America

ISBN:978-1-60604-781-1
1. Self-Help, Personal Growth, Happiness
2. Self-Help, Personal Growth, Self-Esteem
08.11.25

ENDORSEMENTS

"*I'm Not Perfect and It's Okay* is a wonderfully written book, filled with simple life lessons that lead to a place of wisdom. One of the author's greatest gifts is her wisdom, and she shares it beautifully. May you connect with her gentle guidance like I have, for inside these pages is a gift of love."

A. Cockerill, B.A., B.S.W.

"Inspiring and uplifting...each chapter guides you to a place of self acceptance, peace, and happiness!"

C. Lidster, Payroll Coordinator

"Charming, witty, and captivating to the last word! I couldn't put this book down. It warmed my heart and brought tears to my eyes. This book is a treat for everyone. When I read this book, I realized how important it is to make the right choices and also the many lessons we have to learn when we make the wrong ones. An excellent work of art! Share it with your family and friends."

S. Sarafinchan, Executive Administrative Assistant/HR Coordinator

For Fred, our children, and
our grandchildren...*with love*

ACKNOWLEDGMENTS

I would like to thank my husband, Fred, for all his support and guidance in the writing of this book. I could not have done it without him. I would also like to thank our three daughters, Cheryl, Andrea, and Joanna, for reading my manuscript and for being such an inspiration to me in the writing of it. I would like to gratefully acknowledge Andrea for her influence in spurring me on to revisit this dream of mine. I would also like to thank Craig, my son-in-law, for taking the time to read my manuscript before it was edited. As well, I would like to thank John, a lifelong friend of both my husband and myself, for reading my manuscript and writing the foreword for it.

I am grateful to all those who have been in my life, whether in a big way or a small one. Thank you for teaching me all that I know today. By becoming the student, I was able to eventually learn the skills required to be the teacher that I am today. Many years ago when I left classroom teaching and started a new branch of my life, I discovered that no matter what I did, I always seemed to fall back on my teaching skills. I soon realized that once a teacher, always a teacher. This book is the result.

I would also like to thank my sister, Shirley, for asking to read my manuscript and for being so moved by it. She promised that she will read it again once it is polished and published. I look forward to sharing it with the rest of my family as well. I am grateful to my friends and the many acquaintances I have mentioned it to along the way who have shown an interest in reading my book.

I would like to thank Richard Tate, Founder of Tate Publishing & Enterprises, LLC. I loved his welcoming letter and was very touched by his words, "We pray daily for God to send us authors who are anointed with a wonderful word we can share." I am so pleased to have been chosen as one of those authors. I would also like to thank Trinity Tate and Janey Hays (Author Acquisitions) for believing in me as an author. I am also grateful to Dave Dolphin, Rachael Sweeden, and the production team at Tate Publishing. I am truly honored to have this opportunity. I am grateful to my editor, Jaime McNutt Bode, for working on my manuscript with me and for helping me make my book as good as it can possibly be.

Last, but not least, I would like to thank each and every one of you for taking the time to read what I have to say. Although this book was written in recipe form for my children and my grandchildren, I soon came to realize that it may very well be a good recipe for all children. That is the true purpose of this book—to share what I have learned with as many people as possible and hopefully make a positive difference. At last, this part of my dream has been realized!

TABLE OF CONTENTS

FOREWORD

I have had the pleasure of knowing Fred, the author's husband, since we were about three years old. I have known Dolores, the author, for almost as long as Fred has known her. I met her when she was sixteen years old. Suffice it to say that Fred and Dolores have been dear friends for half a century, give or take a few years. I have always admired the strength of their marriage. I have marveled at how they have been able to remain as not only husband and wife but also best friends to one another for so long.

Dolores' book is full of sage advice. I thought of an analogy that sums up the inherent worth of this book. When I was young and was visiting my grandparents on their ranch, I would go out picking Saskatoon berries that my grandmother would preserve or make into pies. Although every berry looked delicious, I dutifully gathered the berries and put them into the pails. Every so often, however, I would come across a berry that was so plump and perfectly ripe that I had to consume it immediately. Dolores' book is much like that experience. The book is chock full of great ideas, advice, and truths, just like all the Saskatoon berries were delicious. Each person who reads the book will find truisms that strike them as being of such immense personal worth that they must be consumed immediately, figuratively speaking. The statements that strike one person as being so meaningful will often be different from those that have such a personal meaning for another. It is up to the individual to select the concepts that strike him as being the gems that they are, but rest assured, each person will find several truths that are of particular worth to him. The reader will find a plethora of great ideas and comments, such that in my opinion, everyone will love this book.

John Matthews, B.A., B. Ed.

AUTHOR'S NOTE

"Four Rooms" is a chapter in my second manuscript, yet to be published, which best explains the use of the quotes I have chosen to use in my books. I am including a short excerpt from this chapter. It goes as follows:

The second room I enjoy visiting on a daily basis is the room where I exercise my intellect. It is the room that I have used to better educate myself, as well as challenge and develop my own intelligence. In this room I can no longer claim that ignorance is bliss. I have chosen to educate myself in such a way that I feel confident in asking questions that at one time I wouldn't have dreamed possible. Finding the courage to do so has increased my faith not only in a loving God but in myself.

Stretching yourself mentally can come in all forms. Although I enjoy reading and playing bridge, one of the forms I especially enjoy is in puzzle form. Over the years, I have taken great pleasure in developing my puzzle solving skills. The more I solve these puzzles, the better I get at it. The better I get at it, the better I feel about myself. My favorite puzzles to solve are crosswords and cryptoquotes. Although they all bring me pleasure, the puzzle that has enhanced my life the most is the cryptoquote. This quote is encoded by mixing up all the letters of the alphabet to mean a different letter in the quote. By figuring out which letter stands for which, you can eventually decode the quote of the puzzle. Every day the code is different. I feel I have been doubly blessed by having both the desire and the ability to do these puzzles. First of all, it makes me feel somewhat intelligent to be able to do them. Secondly and even more importantly, most of the quotes that I have saved and savored over the years are from these puzzles. Some of these wise sayings from some of the greatest thinkers that have ever lived or still live today have been found in these puzzles. Many of them have been said or written by some pretty sage people like Einstein, Confucius, numerous writers, philosophers, past presidents, and the like, which are too numerous to mention by name here. I have had the double pleasure of not only solving these puzzles, but I've personally gained from their sagacity...

Due to the fact that I had no way of knowing how or when I would ever have the opportunity to use these quotes, I have saved them in a very simple way in order to read them at my leisure. I have also saved numerous quotes from motivational calendars, church bulletins, and e-mails over the last several years. The quotes that I have cut out of the newspaper usually come from our Diversion page in the local paper. Others I just cut out from magazines or ripped from calendars so as to not only enjoy them at the time but to keep for future reference, as they brought me so much pleasure. I view these quotes as similar to a stamp or coin collection. I cherish my collection and consider them a valuable asset, although they have no monetary value. In essence, my stash of quotes is priceless to me. I have done my best to now provide a source for all the quotes that I have used in my book. I sincerely hope that you enjoy them as much as I have over the years and that they are able to enhance your life in much the same way that they have enhanced mine.

INTRODUCTION

Today, after many years, I'm going to once again attempt to write a book. I am no author, and right up front I am going to admit that I will be writing in a very unorthodox way. I have always been my own kind of person, and I have decided to do things in my own style. I am going to write from the heart as dictated to me by my own inspiration and personal relationship with God. I will label the chapters as I write them by using one of the special quotes or sayings that I have both saved and savored over the years. Some of these will also be included in the story that I have to tell.

Nowadays, there are so many personal self-help books, but this one is being written to help myself. If by chance your reading this book also helps you, then it will bring me even greater pleasure. It will have served a purpose far greater than I could have ever imagined! However, I want to say at the onset that I agree with Leo Tolstoy when he states that, "It is easier to produce ten volumes on philosophical writing, than to put one principle in practice."[1] Remember these words as you read this book. It takes a lifetime to master the art of living wisely, and it must be learned one step at a time.

This book has been written according to my own personal healing circle. In my opinion, the first step of learning to love yourself is very important. Although I feel that all the steps can add to our lives, there is always a beginning and an end to the healing process. This is where I started on my journey, and I am suggesting that it is a good point to start. After reaching this point, the rest of the steps became clearer to me.

I would have to say that the following three steps are very important as well. I think that up to and including the chapter titled "More F Words," my book would be more beneficial if it was read in this particular order. This is what I consider to be the essential ingredients to the recipe I am offering to better life coping skills. After this point, the suggestions don't necessarily have to follow in order to achieve their full benefit.

At the beginning of several of the chapters, I start by writing in the present. The reason I have chosen to do this is to remind the reader of where I am today in my healing circle. I want to establish where I started and what I did along the way to get to the point of having the desire and inspiration to write this book today. The healing process is a lifelong journey, and even though I have referred to it as a healing circle, it is not what I consider to be a closed circle. In essence, when I was forced to look at my own life in such a way that I knew I required healing, I had to go back in time to what I found to be the root of my problem. When I describe the whole process, right up to the point where I am today, I refer to as my healing circle. I have come to realize that there are more links to be added to it as I continue to grow and learn. As a result, I picture it, more as a chain of circles linked together like a fine gold chain that I cherish more and more each day. Each circle has sad, happy, and fond memories. These circles continue to be linked together to form the chain of my life events.

I would like to also explain a little of the philosophy behind the desire to write my book and the style I have chosen to write it in. Not unlike my husband, I have some French ancestry. Although I would consider my husband's to be greater than mine because his "mother tongue" or first language is French, I learned many French customs and words from my father because his first language was also French. Much to my disappointment, I never fully mastered the ability to speak French and do not consider myself bilingual. I always dreamed that one day I would be able to have a conversation in this much loved language of mine. I never fulfilled this dream, but over the years I became quite adept at understanding some of the vocabulary. I was not able to speak the language well, and the words I could speak I spoke with an English accent. I also had to translate the English word to French in my mind and then speak. This was a slow process.

In French, the word "anglais" means English. My husband always knew of my dream to speak

French, and oftentimes he would anglaisize a French word and insert it into our conversations. I loved they way he did this because it made me feel that I could speak a little French. He would often use the verb "jongler," which means to juggle, in many of these conversations. Many years ago, the jongleur or minstrel was very well known in France. He would travel from town to town and juggle, sing, or tell many long stories in order to entertain his audience.

On completion of my book, you may get a better understanding of my style of writing, because I have told many stories not unlike the olden day jongleur. Oftentimes when I was deep in thought, my husband would ask me what I was jongling about. He could see that I was juggling ideas around in my mind by the expressions on my face. He wanted to know what those thoughts were in order to have a better understanding of me, which would result in a closer relationship.

The information in this book is the result of twenty-five years of jongling. I have now put my thoughts into words so that he, along with all my readers, can actually read what was going on in my mind. I realize that not all people have the desire to read or listen to storytelling, so at the bottom of each chapter I get to the point of what the chapter is about. To the jongleur, the story is the entertainment. To the reader, the points may be of greater or equal enjoyment.

My goal is to demonstrate what I am thinking and to establish the gentle tone I am using. As I am writing this book, I want you to picture yourself sitting across the table from me and having an intimate conversation. The way I write is pretty much the same as the way I talk. Although I am very passionate about my writing, my tone is meant to be soft, gentle, and kind.

Many years ago when one of my daughters was about five years old, she ran into the house while I was sitting at the kitchen table. She wanted to talk to me about something, and I was right in the middle of doing something else. Although I nodded at her while she was speaking, I never looked up. I did hear her voice, but she knew that she did not have my full attention. She gently put her small hand on my face and turned my head toward her so I would really listen to what she had to say. Symbolically speaking, the content of this book can be seen as my hand reaching out to you and gently turning your face toward me so that you can better hear what I am saying. By doing so, you may choose to listen to my voice and learn from it.

THE GREATEST OF
THESE IS LOVE

So many books have been written about God and on the meaning of life. They have been written by theologians, philosophers, psychologists, and many other well educated and deep thinking individuals. I am none of the above, but in some small way, I am all of the above because I have been exposed to many of the teachings through education or experience.

Some books have been read and reread many times over. Some of them have been used in the school system to educate and broaden the minds of students across the world. One of the greatest books ever written is the Bible, which has many authors. Over the years, I have asked myself how these men knew what to write. I have also asked myself when referring to the Bible, why men, at that time, were the only ones with such great inspiration and courage to share their work with all of mankind. I feel that God inspires each and every one of us if we have the desire to listen to the still, small voice that lives within. It is this voice that gets our creative juices flowing and is the inspiration for all the good ideas that come to us in our daily lives.

Over time, I have decided to simplify my life and to look at as many things as possible from this very same point of view. I find that life can become so complex that we can forget the things in life that were meant to bring us the most pleasure. If one goes back to the first teachings of Jesus, the message he was teaching is and always has been very basic and very clear. It is as simple as the kindergarten rule of doing unto others as you would have them do unto you. The theme that most captures my interest in the Bible is about loving God and loving thy neighbor. To me, this is the truth and the only meaningful truth that needs to be adopted in order to answer God's call. Life is a lot simpler than what most of us have made it out to be. It is with this simplistic theme in mind that I will explain some of my views.

The first of these views that I would like to expand upon is love. To me, it is our most basic need. The need to love and to be loved is almost interchangeable, but the hardest person to actually love is oneself.

"Love has two daughters—kindness and patience."[2] It is very important to bear this in mind as I go through the different points that I used to help myself. Important changes take time, and this requires a lot of patience and perseverance. It also requires a big dose of kindness, not only to others but to oneself. "Kindness in words creates confidence. Kindness in thinking creates profoundness. Kindness in giving creates love."[3] Be kind to yourself, and you will learn to be truly kind to others.

So many times throughout life I have met several

people who don't like themselves for one reason or another. I must admit that at times, I have been at the top of the list. We want to be more like someone else, we want to have more of what someone else has, or we just want to be prettier, happier, or more successful. We think other people have more confidence or more self-esteem than us. Over and over again, we compare ourselves to others and come up short.

Very few people actually want to admit this to anyone. It almost seems that if we did, no one could or would want to relate to us. After years of soul searching, sharing, and reading, I have come to realize how much alike we really all are in this regard. In most cases, it seems to come with time, age, and maturity before we actually admit this, not only to ourselves, but to the world around us. By the world around us, I mean our own personal world and some of the more trusted people in it. It would be so much easier if we didn't feel the need to compare ourselves to others and even easier if it didn't matter what other people think, but it does.

So, with this thought in mind, one of the quotes that helped me in my desire to develop self-love is that "You can conquer others with power, but it takes true strength to conquer yourself."[4] Over twenty-five years ago, during a difficult period in my life, I literally forced myself to stand before the mirror and say, "I love you." I had to realize and reaffirm that

God made me in his image and likeness and that he loved me just as I was, flaws and all. The more I accepted this fact, the more I became able to accept others for who they are rather than whom I wanted them to be. I may not always succeed at this, but it is certainly not from lack of trying. When I don't, I remind myself that I am human and that God made me this way for a reason, and I remind myself to keep persevering. Hence, I'm not perfect and it's okay.

At this time, I also felt compelled to get back to the ABCs of my faith. I reflected all the way back to my first encounter with God at the beginning of my formal education, as early as first grade, and how I was taught. I looked at the basic questions that were asked and answered all in one breath. Who made you…God made me. How did God make you…God made me in his image and likeness. Why did God make you…God made me to know, love, and serve the Lord.

This sounds good, yet somehow in the midst of this education, another lesson was also taught. It was the lesson about sin. First, it was the sinfulness of Adam and Eve. Then it was about our own sinfulness at such young ages, told to such impressionable young minds. But even more importantly, it was about original sin and the indelible scar left on all of our souls.

There was no mention of love in those early days. We were taught about hell and eternal damnation. We were taught about mortal sin, venial sin, and dying with a sin on our soul that would never be forgiven if we had not gone to confession. We were taught that God was a punishing and unforgiving Father, and we risked the loss of his love just like Adam and Eve. We were taught a lot of frightening things, but the one thing that sticks in my mind the most is that we were not taught about God's wondrous love and mercy.

If we are made in God's image and likeness like we learned, but he is not seen as loving and kind, then how can we see ourselves that way? This may be my own personal case; however, by reflecting back to what shaped my personality, it gave me some understanding of myself and the negative thoughts and feelings I was living with. How many of us have started off in some similar way? Maybe it is not by the same religious foundation but by other child rearing practices that have had a similar result. How is it possible to have a healthy self-image when one is taught that they have little or no self-worth or that there is so much to fear? Today we can now clearly see the results of such a concept in the need for all the self-help books that are out there. In order to truly heal ourselves we all need to get back to the root of the problem and go from there.

In my early thirties, I was faced with a very serious bout of depression. It was extremely debilitating and filled me with discouragement and despair. In order to start the healing process, I had to understand how

I arrived at this point and what I was going to do about it. It was very difficult to come up with any solutions from this frame of reference.

There seemed to be a genetic predisposition to my depression. I also know that the exposure to the rigid religious views taught to me at such a young age had a huge impact. It was like my past education had come back to haunt me. I remember when I was six years old, I would twist my hair with my little fingers in a childlike trance to try to bring some kind of soothing and solace to myself as I dwelled upon the concept of hell and what would happen to me if I wasn't good. I remember the black robes that the sisters and the priests wore in those days and how frightened I was of them and all that they were saying. At the age of six, I would picture the concept of hell and the magnitude of the words eternal suffering in my mind and try to make sense of what was being said. I listened to and absorbed these words and believed everything that I heard. I cannot underestimate the unbelievable fear that was instilled in me, whether it was meant to be or not. I would like to believe that my teachers' motives were good and that they were just repeating the way that they had been taught.

Many children were unaffected by these teachings, but I know others who have been deeply affected, not unlike myself. It all depended on the personality of the child. I was very sensitive and shy, and I believed absolutely everything verbatim. It never entered my mind to think otherwise. I was also taught that to question anything was to demonstrate a lack of faith.

Initially, and still to this day, I find this a very difficult subject to discuss. It is much easier for me to write about it rather than to talk about it. Although I have used the word easier, it has by no means been easy. The impact it had on my life and the lives of my family still brings tears to my eyes. As I have gone back in time, I have forced myself to remember some pretty painful things. It is not so much about myself and my past depression, but it was necessary to evoke memories of people who have been so dear to me and are no longer here on earth. At times, as I do this, my eyes well up with tears that eventually run down my cheeks as I relive some of these moments. Other times I break out in a smile as I recall lighter and happier ones. I am so grateful for these happy times.

I feel the need to say that depression feels very different from other physical ailments, at least from my personal point of view. It is generally not well received, and not all people have empathy with the condition. Several people think that you can just "snap out of it," and this only adds to the frustration of trying to live with it. In my instance, it felt that I was somehow responsible for my depressed state. Perhaps it happens and I am unaware of it, but I can't image anyone suggesting that a person suffering from diabetes, cancer, or some other life altering illness "snap out" of what they are going through. Getting angry and frustrated with a depressed person only further aggravates and exacerbates the condition. He/she is having enough trouble trying to cope with life as it is. I am not trying to criticize, condemn, or complain. This is not my goal, nor has it ever have been. I only want to share because I care. I am not looking for pity for such a crippling condition but rather for compassion for all those who suffer in silence. I am also seeking compassion for those who live with a depressed person and, last but not least, compassion for those who have added to the crippling effect of the condition by their innocence or their ignorance. My silence no longer feels golden. It is time to find the courage to share my healing circle with my family, my friends, and all of you who choose to embrace what I have written.

During a depressed state, you feel very alone and isolated. As stated above, in most instances you will not find the compassion you might get when experiencing other illnesses. You, therefore, might try to cover up what you are experiencing, and you may become further depressed. As a result, you may feel even more isolated in this downward spiral until you reach the point when you can hardly get up in the morning to start your day. You can lose your zest for life, your sense of humor, and joy for the little things that once enhanced your life and brought you so much pleasure.

A bout with major depression is like living in a black pit. Each day you have to work very hard at climbing out of it in order to see the light of dawn. It is at this time, when you may feel the need draw from a Higher Power to give you the strength and courage to face each new day. I found that without my faith there would have been very little hope to ever rise above the depressed state, not only faith in God but learning to have a renewed faith in myself. This is the hardest task because a depressed person has usually lost faith and trust in himself/herself. It is almost impossible to draw strength from a well that has run so dry. Eventually, by taking small steps and being satisfied with small gains, you can make some deposits into this dry well. Due to the fact that there is so little left to draw from, the only choice you actually have is to try to replenish it so you can make your way back to a full and rewarding life.

At this time, I was filled with guilt, confusion, and trepidation. I visited a priest whom I had known for almost my entire life to try to get some kind of spiritual guidance and emotional support. During this very trying and emotional time, and due to his lack of understanding of my situation, he chose to shun me after he told me that, "I'd better reconcile myself to God." I had many confused thoughts, and I'm sure I wasn't making much sense in trying to express them. His response further added to my guilt, fear, and already depressed state. It took me over a year to get back on my feet. I needed the time to think this situation through more effectively. Initially, and many times afterward, I thought I was being punished like the way I had been taught because I had done something so displeasing to God; however, I never knew quite what it was. I kept searching for answers. I read with a vengeance to try to comprehend what was happening to me.

I must admit that this was the most difficult period of my life thus far. I had left my teaching career in order to recuperate, and I could not get the courage to return. It felt like I had failed miserably. I felt so lost. I then decided that in order to continue pursuing work outside our home, I would have to make some major decisions about what I was going to do in this regard. I had to learn how to think outside the box.

I came to realize that I didn't need a classroom to teach. Classrooms have walls, but teaching doesn't only need to take place inside those walls. I decided to change careers, and I got hired by a major financial institution. I soon discovered that before I could teach again, I had to be a student and learn totally new information. It took some time, and it was no easy task.

Six months into the job, much to my dismay, I had a relapse. I pulled myself up again and returned to work after six weeks. Once I regained my self-esteem and self-respect, I was able to use some of my teaching skills in my new job. I enrolled in some courses being offered and made every effort to re-educate myself. Several people in my new place of employment saw the benefits of my previous teaching experience, and they helped me utilize them in a totally different situation. I will be forever grateful to all those people who helped me along the way. In most instances, they had absolutely no idea of what had happened or the point of reference I was coming from. Although they knew I had been on sick leave, they had no idea I suffered from depression or my previous history with it.

This is just my story, but each and every one of us has one. It doesn't necessarily have to do with depression.

For me, by going back in time, looking at myself, and striving to better myself, I learned so much more. It not only gave me personal insight, it also gave me a better understanding of others. The more I saw and understood my own shortcomings and virtues, the more I understood and accepted others.

As difficult and as negative as the above experience was for me, in retrospect I would not have wanted it any other way. When I was in the midst of it, I prayed and wished it away. After much soul searching and hard work, I accepted myself and realized that it is human to fail, and I could get up again. I also learned that life can consist of many failures, but each and every time, you just have to keep getting up. For me, it was easier to fall down and get up rather than just lay there and suffer with bouts of depression.

When I learned to look at myself this way, I also learned to look at others in the same light. At times it is hard to measure up to the goals we all set for each other or for ourselves. We all fail at one time or another. By seeing myself in a more human light and in a more humane way, I learned that the person I was had nothing to do with whether I failed at something. I could still be considered a good person, no matter what was going on in my life.

This is when I learned to separate the person from the action. Although I had not completely succeeded at classroom teaching, I was not being punished for not being good the way I had been taught. Being good at something and being a good person are two totally different things, but it is very hard to accept this fact if you have been taught otherwise. Oftentimes people associate suffering with punishment. It was ingrained in me that I would be punished if I stepped out of line. I have come to realize that there are many innocent people who do not deserve to suffer and therefore are not being punished.

After experiencing all that I did, I soon learned that I am not perfect and that failure is a fact of life. I was not being punished either. I also learned that when you look at your whole self and decide what you like or don't like, you can alter your own behavior. I did this by looking back at what caused all my confused thinking, religious hang ups, and guilt. I knew that it didn't start in my early thirties. It merely peaked there. It had a much earlier origin, and I needed to go all the way back to figure it out. I knew what brought me to my knees had to do with religion, but I needed to know why. The only solution was to go as far back in my memory bank that I could and get to the root of the problem. That's exactly what I did. I had to start with the ABC's of my original instruction and go from there. Once I did this, I understood myself a whole lot better. Once I understood myself better, I also had more understanding for human nature period. I just had to start with the human I needed to know better, namely, myself.

I have come to the conclusion that it is from this well of understanding that we find empathy and compassion for the world around us. Our own world is a microcosm of the whole world. If we cannot find peace in this small world where we live, there will never be world peace. How can we expect such a thing if we cannot make it work on such a small scale?

So let's get back to looking in the mirror. If you don't like yourself, ask yourself why. If the reason is because of the way that you were taught, acknowledge and embrace that fact. However, there can be many reasons for not liking ourselves. Possibly we lack education and feel inadequate. We can feel inferior for a number of reasons, including a poor self-image due to body weight, shape, or size. Sometimes we don't feel smart enough, regardless of our education. Some of us may feel that we have been born on the wrong side of the tracks, while others may feel that their skin is the wrong color or they are lesser because of their sex. Others may not be proud of their heritage or their own personal backgrounds and family history.

If a person has nagging feelings of inferiority that affect his/her quality of life, that person is the only one that can answer the questions about what is causing their own personal situation. In most instances, the remedy or solution to the problem can be the same, because in the end, the goal is to overcome the feelings of inferiority or inadequacy by developing better life coping skills. After you have done this, though, there is plenty of work to be done. This is not about blame, but more about understanding ourselves. Remember, the better we understand ourselves and accept ourselves for what we are, the more we will understand and accept others for who they are. One very important fact to remember is that in most instances, our parents, educators, and mentors actually taught us the very things that they were taught and in much the same way. Education is a process that evolves and slowly changes with time. The key to life and what love is all about lies in accepting this. Education comes in a variety of forms. Not all education is formal, but we are constantly on the learning curve by observing, learning, and being influenced by others.

Love really is very simple. In fact, it needs no words or language at all. It can be a special feeling, look, touch, or act of charity, humility, or generosity. God lives in each and every one of us. God is perfect love. If you strive for perfect love, you will learn to see the face of God in your spouse, your children, and your fellow human. This should be our goal as humankind. If and when we do this, a lot of our problems will be solved. However, charity really does begin at home, so once again start with the face in the mirror. I encourage everyone to go have a really good look at yourself. Look right into your own eyes and into the depth of your own soul. It's not as easy as you think!

Learn to love yourself as you are...that's the first step.

A SIMPLE GENIUS, A
GENTLE PHILOSOPHER

Well...did you take that look in the mirror? Maybe I should have suggested that you do it figuratively rather than literally. I know how hard it is to do such a thing; however, I do believe it is very important. I call it getting to the root of the problem, and I believe it is a problem because there wouldn't be such a need for all the self-help books if it weren't.

I shared the first chapter I wrote with one of my daughters, and she told me what she liked best about it. She said that she liked the simplicity and the fact that it was easy to digest. Thanks to her input, I've decided to write this chapter next. I remember a cute story that took place many years ago when I started teaching school. Every year, our school would have an annual tea held sometime in the spring. It was a large school, and all the teachers were involved, as well as a lot of parents. The teachers either volunteered to do different tasks or the principal would often assign some. It was a lot of work. Of course, there usually was a theme to these teas, with all the decorations to go with it. It was quite a grand affair. The teacher chosen to select the theme did something I found very amusing at the time, although I must admit the principal did not find it nearly as amusing.

Shortly before the day of the tea, when all the

hustle and bustle to do with it arrived, the principal was checking things out and was quite alarmed to see that there were no decorations going up. When he asked the teacher where they were, she said that she had chosen the theme simplicity, and there would be none that year. Well, I figure she was one teacher ahead of her time because in no time flat, the principal made sure that everything was decorated. I'm sure that teacher will never know how much she made my day! I can't even remember her name, yet I do believe she had the right idea. She just wanted to keep things simple instead of all the planning and running around to make a success out of something that could have been done in a much simpler way.

This example shows two different ways of looking at the same thing. According to the teacher, the purpose of the annual tea was to end the school year on a positive note. It was about working together and sharing a day with parents, fellow staff members, and students. It would seem that to the administrator that the appearance of how things looked carried more weight. In essence, their goals were quite different.

I agree with the teacher's assessment of the situation. To me, it was far more about the enjoyment of the occasion rather than about themes and decorations. In fact, by focusing on a theme, it actually took away from the enjoyment because it added more work at an already stressful time of the year from a teacher's point of view. Decorations and themes seem to be more about giving a good impression. It's one of the reasons I have chosen to write this book in a very simple way. I'm not trying to impress anyone. What I am trying to accomplish here is to share some philosophical ideas over a simple cup of tea, symbolically speaking. I prefer to eliminate the fanfare and keep it simple rather than formal. I feel that too much fanfare can be a distraction and take from, rather than add to, the theme of what is being said. "The world's great men have not commonly been great scholars, nor its great scholars, great men."[5] I'm no scholar, nor am I a man; I'm only trying to share the steps I have used over the last twenty-five years to enhance my own life and the lives of those around me.

In the last chapter, I mentioned the still, small voice that lives within. It is this voice that has guided me throughout my life. Although I feel it is a part of my most basic being, I also feel it is apart from me in the sense that it is the essence of my soul and actually wiser than me. It seems that I am able to draw from a well that is deeper than my own. I believe it is where we gather our best wisdom. "There is a Divinity that shapes our ends...but we can help by listening for its voice."[6]

I have come to refer to this voice as the simple genius and the gentle philosopher. It has brought me great solace to describe what I hear this way. All those years ago, when I was doing so much reflecting,

I came to realize that what lay within me could be a friend or foe depending on how I looked at it. How I chose to look at myself and those around me had a huge impact on my life. I decided that in order to reshape my life, I had to improve my self-image. Although I wasn't always thoroughly pleased with what I saw, if I dealt with one thing at a time, it was much more manageable. At first I was so hard on myself, but then I chose to give myself a break. I decided to befriend my inner buddy. Instead of being my own worst enemy, I decided I would be my own best friend. The voice that I heard ever so softly helped teach me to do things this way. Without this inner guidance, I would not be who I am today.

I'm going to recommend a little exercise here. It doesn't take very long and is well worth the effort. Choose a person you love and admire. At the top of one side of a blank piece of paper, write this person's name. Draw a line and then write your own name at the top of the other side. Now under this person's name, write down all the things that you actually admire and respect about them. I bet the list is pretty long. Now on the other side of the paper, write down the things you admire and respect about yourself. Ten to one, there are a lot less virtues on your side of the paper than on the other. If this is true, it does not need to stay that way. This is where you, as your own best friend, get down to work.

This is the time where we discover that "what we

are is God's gift to us. What we become is our gift to God."[7] The simple genius that lies within us can teach us so much about ourselves. All we need to do is listen and take the advice that is being offered. We all have this power, but we don't always tap into it. Now is a good time to do just that. We must sit back in silence and listen.

When focusing on the best qualities of great people, you have the opportunity to adopt their standards and values. In this way, you have a wonderful chance to experience your own greatness by emulating their behavior. So, you know that person you admired and respected in the previous paragraph? Perhaps he or she is the one to emulate. In this way, instead of beating yourself up, you take one small step to strive to have the virtues that you see and admire most in that person. Start small with something that you can accomplish. By doing so, you can have many successes and help improve how you view yourself. This habit is a positive endeavor to be all that you can be.

Although the first step of this process, as stated in the first chapter, is to love yourself, it is necessary to admit that there are some things we just don't like about ourselves. By admitting this, we are given the power to make the necessary changes in a positive way. The key here is to realize that loving and liking are two different emotions. My goal is to try to differentiate between the two. Most of us have a person or several people in our lives whom we love. In my experience, even though I can feel love for these people, they may engage in a behavior or a set of behaviors that I do not always like. When I look at myself, I see things the same way. I know that I am a lovable person, but I also can engage in behavior that I do not like or even respect. When I look at myself this way, I make every effort to separate the two emotions. Admitting I don't like something about myself, or anyone else for that matter, does not diminish my love. The only power I actually have in this situation is over myself. When I see something I don't like, I have the power to change it. It doesn't mean to say I will love myself more. It merely means that I can cease engaging in a particular behavior if I have the desire to do so. The more you work at this, the easier it gets. This is how you gradually change the face in the mirror into one that you can not only love but like and respect. Even the smallest change in yourself will create a change in someone close to you. One of these changes could be as simple as deciding to smile more and making a concentrated effort to do so. Before you know it, so many people will be smiling back at you. Trust me on this one; it really works! Keep it simple. You can't find anything much simpler than a genuine smile. "A smile is rest to the weary, daylight to the discouraged, sunshine to the sad, and natures best antidote for trouble."[8]

So now sit back and take time to digest all the

information you have processed. You can only do this in silence because it is the only way that you can hear what is being said! Remember, God still speaks to those who listen. These are very sage words and should not be taken lightly.

Step 2 Take time to listen to the simple genius and the gentle philosopher that lives within you.

LISTEN UP SOME MORE!

Well, friend or foe...what's it going to be?

For fear of sounding like a broken record, I will try not to sound too repetitive. It's just that some things need to be said more than once in order to realize their full importance. I realize that I am using the word "listen" in both this chapter and the last one to stress what I want to say.

To me there is a subtle difference between hearing and actually listening. We can hear all kinds of words, music, sounds, noise, and so on in our everyday lives. Our ears pick up sound waves all day long. In my opinion, listening is a totally different thing than hearing. It is more about the process of deciphering what has been heard and really listening for the message and what it may mean to you. For example, the sound of music can be very enjoyable, but choosing to listen to and interpret the lyrics can bring even greater joy. I think it is possible to hear all kinds of sounds without delving deeper to find out more. Listening is more of a desire to understand some of the sounds or voices that we hear in order to get a better appreciation for what is being said or heard.

Not all sounds are worth listening to. Some can be loud and obnoxious with no message at all. Others can be quiet and soothing, while others are powerful and impressionable. Listening can often inspire you to act on what you've heard. In my opinion, it's good to hear, but you can be hearing impaired and still know how to listen. This is the reason I am devoting two chapters to the art of listening.

I remember reading a story in a church bulletin quite some time ago, and it has stuck in my mind ever since. Of course it is not a true story, but one of the best ways to get a message across is in the form of a story. This is the same technique that was used by Jesus in his day. Aesop's fables are another well-known example of getting a message across using this format.

There once was a man who lived in a village that was being flooded. As the water started to rise, he moved up a level in his house. On the first day, a boat with rescuers came around to pick up those who were stranded. This man refused to go with them, saying that the Lord would save him. The water continued to rise, and he had to move up another flight in his house. On the second day, another attempt was made to rescue him, and he repeated the same thing as the day before, that God would save him. On the third day, he was forced onto the roof by the flood and still refused to get into the boat when it came by. On that day, however, after he refused to go with the rescuing party, the water rose even more, and he drowned. When he met St. Peter, he was pleased to see that he had made it to heaven, but he was upset that he had not been saved on earth. St. Peter said that he had no reason to be disappointed because three times God had sent someone for him and three times he had refused.

I believe the moral of this story is that God not only speaks to us as individuals, he also speaks to us through other people. So although it is necessary to listen to our own inner voice, we must also be open to the people God puts into our lives to guide us. This is how we learn to use the gift of discernment. It takes time to hone the skill of combining the two, but both involve more effective listening. As stated in the first paragraph of this chapter, listening, in my opinion, can be considered more of an action word. It may mean doing something with the information that you have received, whether it is verbal or nonverbal. It is actually the process of trying to make more sense out of a message in order to give it more meaning. It's a form of reading between the lines or seeing the writing on the wall. Listening requires letting ideas, thoughts, etc., sink in and utilizing your intellect to figure things out. Therefore, listening requires analytical thinking.

It's important that we choose people that we respect and admire to listen to. "A good listener is not only popular everywhere, but after a while he knows something."[9] You cannot underestimate the voice of experience. It is wise to listen to those around us whom we trust and those who may have been exposed to more facets of life than we have. It's taking the time to really look around at the people in your life and asking yourself whom you would want to be most like. What rules have they used to guide themselves? Why would you want to be more like them? What do you see? Do you see faith, peace, contentment, genuine happiness, and so on? Are these the things that you value in your life? If so, endeavor to have more of these kind people in your life to guide you. They may not necessarily be older or more educated than you; they may just have had more exposure to life's experiences. There are not enough years in a person's life to experience everything, and those with common sense don't want to. It is the wise who learn from other people's experience in order to deal with the everyday ups and downs of their own lives. Remember, "Genius is entitled to respect only when it promotes the peace and improves the happiness of mankind."[10] So I suggest that you ask yourself, "What kind of friend am I, and what kind of friend do I want to be in my life?"

You must also remember that the habits most valued by society are not always the ones most valued by God. To really become all that you dream to be, you must be prepared to be different from a lot of other people. Most people struggle with this concept. At first this may be very difficult to deal with, but in time you will learn to celebrate your own uniqueness. Although we are all alike in many ways, we must also strive to maintain our individuality. This is just my opinion, but in order to truly make a difference in life, you need to be different.

I recall a cute little question that I heard once. What is the difference between a diamond and a cubic zirconium? Actually, they are both the same! They are both just shiny pieces of glass. In most instances the difference can only be seen with intense scrutiny, and it actually takes the expertise of a jeweler to see it. The only thing that gives the diamond more value is the fact that it is rarer. So my advice to you is to be your own best friend, choose your friends wisely, and dare to be different than the majority of people. This is how you learn to be a diamond in the rough. It has been said that, "a single conversation across the table with a wise man/woman is worth a month's reading of books."[11] You could be that person, but first you must be the student and learn. The student only becomes the teacher after honing the art of listening!

I hope that you have gathered that both kinds of listening are equally important. They require trust on both fronts: trust in yourself based on your own good judgment and personal experience and trust in those you have chosen to have in your life. It is the combination of the two that will bring us the peace, contentment, and happiness that we are actually searching for. Once you achieve this, your priorities will be clearer and easier to attain because you will realize what is important and in what direction you want your life to go. It's making this decision that

really takes time. Life's choices become clearer after
you do this.

Once you are more focused, life really does get
less complicated. Remember the simplicity theme!
The easiest way to a happier life is to keep it simple.
According to Goethe, "a reasonable man only needs to
practice moderation to find happiness."[12] Moderation
and simplicity go hand in hand. So try to keep things
simple and balanced in your life in order for it to all
fall into place. It is not easy to have an uncomplicated
life. As simple as we may want to keep things in our
lives, there are many forces that we have absolutely
no control over; however, at times, we can create
much of the imbalance and unhappiness that we end
up facing.

Oftentimes, it is easier for an outsider to see what
the problem is in another person's life. I don't know
how many times I've heard the expression, "I could
see that coming." When someone is not directly
involved in a burdensome situation, they can be far
more objective and see things clearer. It's at times like
these that more effective listening plays a vital role in
our lives. In a lot of instances, a relative, spouse, or
close friend could be trying to steer you away from
trouble or a perilous situation. It is at these times
that we may have the opportunity to listen to the
words or cues that are being offered.

When our lives are well balanced and less
complicated, we are more open to the receiving

of this guidance. When our lives are stressful and overcomplicated, we are less open to any suggestions or advice from others. It's not to say that people who choose to live a moderate, more balanced life are not ever in need of guidance or are always willing to listen. It's only to say that people who are really stressed out find that the guidance being offered, at times, adds to their already stressful situation. It's almost impossible to listen to anyone at this point because there is a tendency to have too many people trying to help out. The wisest choice here is to never get to that point if you can help it. Yes, simplicity, moderation, balance, and listening all go hand in hand. If you don't practice the first three, however, you may not have the full potential to benefit from the fourth, that of the art of listening.

So thus far we have learned that it is best to love ourselves and listen to our inner voice. This is done in moments of deep silence. We have also learned that it is best to have an inner circle of people whom we trust and respect.

Step 3 Choose your friends wisely and take the time to listen to them and digest what they have to say.

MORE F WORDS!

My goodness, where in the world could I be going now? F words! Admit it, you thought of the unmentionable word. No need to worry about that. First, we learned about deciding whether to be our own friend or foe. Obviously, they both start with an "F." Now the other two "F" words we are going to discuss are about forgiving and being forgiven.

Once again, I will tell a little story. This is actually a true story. I usually try to let you know which ones are real and which ones aren't. In most cases, it doesn't make much difference, because I tell the story to make a point. I will continue to use either format as the need arises to get any given point across. This story revolves around some information told to me by my father shortly before his death. My dad was only sixty-nine years old when he passed away, but he had suffered quite a lot from ill health over the years. He had his first heart attack in his early forties, followed by a stroke in his fifties. Diabetes and some depression also exacerbated his condition. Needless to say, there were times when my dad didn't have a lot of fun, especially in his mid to late sixties. He was a man who spent quite a bit of time in his rocking chair and did a lot of thinking in those last few years of his life.

My dad knew he didn't have much time left and

loved to visit with his children. I would go over often and listen to all he had to say. One day he shared with me that he had gone over his life and had forgiven all the people who had hurt him with the exception of one. He felt really bad about this, as he did not want to meet his maker with an unforgiving heart. He really struggled in this regard. He also told me that many years earlier, when he started to lose so many of his brothers to cancer, while visiting one of them on his death bed in the hospital, my dad had asked him for forgiveness. By doing so, my dad wanted to make sure that he was also forgiven for any of his wrongdoings.

Those were two small instances in his life where he knew he needed to forgive and also knew that he needed to be forgiven. There are only two choices when it comes to forgiveness. Either you are on the giving end or on the receiving end. There is no in between. No matter what, throughout a lifetime, we will alternate many times between the two ends!

Most of us want to be on the end where we do the forgiving because it means we have been wronged and see ourselves as right. Others are forever saying they are sorry and are in constant need of forgiveness. But I can assure you that most people's lives are a balance between the two.

After I left teaching, I was employed by a major financial institution. I worked with a woman whose mother-in-law was dying of cancer. She was really suffering, and my co-worker would go often to visit her in the hospital. One day, one of the nurses called her aside and suggested she tell her mother-in-law that she forgave her. My fellow worker didn't really think she needed to forgive her for anything, but the nurse explained to her that as much as this woman was suffering, she couldn't seem to find the peace and comfort to just let go. The nurse further explained that it had been her experience that some people just needed to be reassured that they were forgiven, and once they heard those words, they would let go. Sure enough, shortly after she was forgiven by her daughter-in-law, the cancer patient settled down and was able to die peacefully. This proves that we cannot underestimate the power of forgiveness in our lives, whether on the receiving end or the giving end. I have no idea about the kind of relationship my fellow employee had with her mother-in-law. It could very well be that she needed to be forgiven by my co-worker because this woman knew she had some how wronged her. I found that the most refreshing aspect to this story was her lack of knowledge about any ill-will between the two of them. Her dying mother-in-law seemed to be seeking forgiveness, according to the nurse on duty. My fellow employee listened to her advice and offered it, although she was somewhat uncomfortable in doing so.

I was very impressed with the kindness that she showed her mother-in-law. If there was any ill-will between the two of them, it was certainly not on her part. She forgave her mother-in-law only as an act of love and kindness in order to release her from the pain she was suffering. In this way, she actually enabled her to rest comfortably and die in peace.

I was very impressed by both the woman who told me the story and by the nurse as well for taking to time to guide my co-worker. She did this out of concern for her patient. She recognized the need to be forgiven in this situation. Whether it was her daughter-in-law who actually needed to forgive her, I will never know. One thing I do know is that in the end, the desired result took place. The forgiveness offered was an act of love. In my opinion, that is what forgiveness is all about.

At this time, I would ask you, my readers, to bear with me as I sometimes confuse the word forgiving with forgiveness. Sometimes I find it very difficult to differentiate between the two, but I will make every effort to do so in the following stories. Although I realize that I may have used some words incorrectly, the main essence of my book is to try and look at life in a more philosophical and kinder way.

As previously mentioned, I saw how hard my dad struggled with his desire to forgive and his inability to do so in that one particular instance. I'm sure he worked at it until his dying moment, as it bothered him so. Sitting across the kitchen table from my dad was a valuable learning experience for me. Over the years, I had many opportunities to learn from his life lessons. He was very eager to share them with me, and I was an eager and willing student. He had some of the neatest expressions, and after he would share a story or an idea with me, he would look right at me and ask, "Do you catch my drift?" It seemed to be his way of ensuring that I knew exactly what he meant. If I didn't, I would ask him some questions, and he would elaborate some more.

My dad and I had a very unique relationship. He loved to share his views with me because he knew how much I loved and respected him. I learned to value what he said and made every effort to try and benefit from his experiences and his words of wisdom. Over time he came to value what I had to say in much the same way.

When my dad chose to discuss the topic about his inability to forgive with me, I knew he was very troubled. I was the one who took the time to reassure and advise him in this particular instance. In "The Greatest of These is Love," I referred to education as a process that evolves and slowly changes with time. As a young child, I was always the student and continued in this role for many years. As I matured and had the opportunity to better educate myself, there were times when I realized I knew some things that my dad didn't know or understand.

My dad had very little formal education. He was what I would call "street smart." I was more "book smart" because I had more formal education. Over the years we learned to share and combine the two, and these became very educational tools to us both. Sometimes we just reversed roles like we had often done before, and I explained my views to him. I had many opportunities to be the teacher over the years, and he became the willing student. I could never have become the teacher if I hadn't been the student first. This process allowed us both to continue to grow and educate each other right up to the end of his life.

We discussed the topics of both the need to forgive and the need to accept forgiveness. I expounded on my philosophy that some people have the tendency to see themselves as the victims or the offended ones. I further explained that more often than not, many people have no idea that they have even offended us. While we sit there in a state of turmoil, not knowing what to do with our hurt feelings, the offenders go on their merry way. I added that depending on what is going on in our lives, we can take greater offense and feel we have more to forgive than we actually do.

The person whom my father had so much trouble forgiving was very well known to me. I took the opportunity to not so much defend but to explain this person's way of doing things. I wanted my dad to realize that so many times in life we unintentionally hurt each other. The key word here is "unintentionally." I felt that this particular person had done just that. I tried to make my dad see that to forgive a person who had unintentionally hurt him was far easier than to forgive one who had purposefully done so. In reality, I wanted my dad to look at the situation more logically and less emotionally so that he could better cope with it.

In my own healing circle, I have used this concept in an untraditional way. According to my knowledge of a healing circle, it usually involves the offended (person needing to forgive) and the offender (person in need of forgiveness, albeit, unaware at times). In the above instance, my dad was the offended person unable to forgive his offender. I could have suggested to my dad that he could do things in the traditional way and approach his offender and explain the situation and his reasons for being offended. On such occasions, after discussing the problem, ideally the offender takes responsibility for causing the pain or hurt feelings and asks to be forgiven. At this point, the offended person (my dad in this particular instance) forgives.

I personally have tried to use the healing circle this way many times in my life; however, it doesn't always work. The person who has supposedly offended you may not be around anymore, or he/she may be unwilling to assume the responsibility of validating the hurt feelings and apologizing for the pain it may have caused. When involving the other person/persons into the circle, you can, at times, give them further power to hurt you. They may not want to own up to what you are saying, and this will further add to your grief. In my healing circle, I discovered that the only real power I have is over myself. Therefore, I encouraged my dad to deal with his situation in much the same way.

I would like to think that I made some small difference in bringing my dad the peace of mind he was looking for at this time in his life. He knew that he was dying, and he wanted to get this off his chest. I also took the time to explain that we too are in need of forgiveness from engaging in the exact same unintentional hurtful behavior. As I further discussed this topic with him, I went on to say that it is extremely hard to truly forgive, but it is equally hard to accept forgiveness. If we do, it is admitting that somehow we have offended another person, and we do not cherish the idea of seeing ourselves in this light. I wanted my dad to realize that all of us unintentionally hurt others at one time or another, and hopefully these people will forgive us for our unintentional hurtful words or actions as well.

I recall a particular occasion in my own life where a person gave me a bouquet of flowers and said that they forgave me. I quickly said thank you, but I must admit I was somewhat taken aback. Even to this day, I have no idea what the person was forgiving me for, but I accepted their forgiveness nonetheless. I just smiled inwardly as I thought to myself, I will take all the forgiveness I can get. I had already come to the conclusion that I'm not perfect and it's okay. If it made this person feel better, that was fine with me.

I'm not so sure that everybody chooses to look at life this way. It was very clear to me that this person, whom I loved very much, had come to the end of a healing circle and was ready to fully embrace me. Forgiving me was part of this circle. At this time I was once again able to draw discernment from the still, small voice that by now had become so familiar to me. This was a moment when silence was the most effective way to communicate. I was very happy that this person had made it to this point in life and had healed enough to forgive me, whether I knew why or not. The point that mattered to me the most was allowing this person to find the same kind of peace I wanted my dad to know. It really wasn't about me. It was not about my healing circle at all, but more about my desire and joy to share in her/his healing.

I realized some time ago that the best way to learn how to forgive is to look to the Master of forgiving for forgiveness. This is when you go back to the mirror and have that really good look at yourself yet again. There is no one alive on this earth today that is not in need of some degree of forgiveness. Not you, not I, nor anyone else that we respectively know is not in need at one time or another. When we truly realize this and ask for and accept our own personal forgiveness, then and only then will we know how to forgive others. That's the conundrum; first we must accept our own weaknesses and need for forgiveness to better accept and forgive others for theirs.

I'm sure a lot of you have heard that little joke about how standing in a church no more makes you a Christian than standing in a garage makes you a car. Perhaps I shouldn't have described this saying as a joke because Laurence J. Peter may not have meant it as one, although it can be presented that way. From my point of view, there have been plenty of times when certain behavior proves to me that it is no laughing matter. To go to church, Sunday after Sunday, and to live a life that's void of forgiveness is the living proof. Forgiveness starts with asking and accepting it for ourselves! After that, it is much easier.

So first and foremost, accept your own need to be forgiven. If you have the need to go to church to reinforce that fact, then please do so. There are many people who don't need to do this, and that's okay too. You can still be a good Christian without standing in a church. The church is just a building, not unlike a garage. It's the action outside the building that really counts. So accept forgiveness for yourself, and you will be eager to forgive others.

I want to share some information from an article that I found in a local newspaper many years ago. I taped it in my red scribbler, and it has become yellow with age. The treasures that I have tucked away to be enjoyed at my leisure have been saved over a long period of time. I have no idea how long I have had this particular article, but it was written by Robert Muller on forgiveness, to be enjoyed by all readers. If I'm not mistaken, I discovered it in an advice column, and I have referred to it many times over to better help me learn the art of forgiveness. I do not know if this is the entire article or just a part of it, as it is a paper clipping and has no heading. I merely cut out the part of the article that was of interest to me.

In one particular paragraph, Robert Muller states that the first step that a person must take is to decide to forgive. He goes on to describe all the negative emotions that arise from not forgiving, with resentment at the top of the list. According to him, "resentment is poisonous and diminishes and devours the self."[13] It can be very difficult to take the first step toward forgiving, but it is the biggest step.

As mentioned in the first chapter when I told you my story about my depression, I mentioned that there was one very important fact to remember. It was about learning to forgive those who taught me about guilt and fear and all the negative consequences following those teachings. But I also know from my own experience that you cannot take this first step until you embrace your own weaknesses and accept forgiveness for yourself.

It was at this point of my life when I fully accepted my own shortcomings. It would seem that I had come to believe that I needed to be perfect to be loved. If you look at failure as a shortcoming and a weakness, you can see yourself as far less than perfect. I had every desire to have a deeper, more intimate relationship with God and to know that his love was not conditional. I never fully knew the meaning of true love or unconditional love. My previous relationship with God was based on fear more than anything else. I feared the loss of his love because that was the only concept that I knew. I needed to admit that I was confused when it came to my perception of my Creator. Regardless of what caused this misconception, I wanted to take responsibility for it. I wanted a loving and fearless relationship with my Maker. I needed to be forgiven for seeing God in such an unhealthy way. I discovered that perfect love truly does cast out fear. I accomplished this by discarding the notion of doing the right thing because I was afraid of being punished if I didn't. I also discarded the notion of doing the right things in life to gain some kind of heavenly reward. I merely wanted to be pleasing to God and to love him/her in the same way that I now felt loved. It seemed to me that the earlier way that God was described to me would be the last way that any of us would want to be depicted. God is perfect love. Period!

In the final analysis, this philosophy coincided with my desire to see life in a simpler way. This act of reaching out to God on such a personal level has brought me untold pleasure. After this, it was much easier to offer the same kind of forgiveness that I had received. As much as humanly possible, I also tried my best to offer the same kind of love that I felt in my own relationship with God. God always was, always is, and always will be. God does not change. Only our perception of him/her does if we have the desire to educate ourselves and be more open to the spiritual evolution of thought that unfolds.

Once you take this first step, "you will see happiness bloom on the face of your human brother or sister,"[14] according to Muller. Over and over again in this article, he stresses the importance to be the first to forgive others and to not wait until they step forward to forgive you. I truly like the part where he emphasizes that "by forgiving you become the master of fate, the fashioner of life, the doer of miracles."[15] I also could not agree with him more when he writes that "to forgive is the highest, most beautiful form of love, in return you will receive untold peace and happiness."[16]

Robert Muller goes on to provide a program for achieving a truly forgiving heart. He starts off the week on Sunday by once again stressing the need to start with yourself, that is to say, start by forgiving yourself. He then continues to go through the days of the week and says to forgive "your family, your friends and associates[17]" and so on throughout the week until you have forgiven "across economic, cultural and political[18]" lines.

I was also very impressed with what Laurence Sterne wrote. The comment that impressed me the most was this one: "Only the brave know how to forgive. A coward never forgives. It is not in his nature."[19] Most people don't realize that it takes a lot of courage to forgive. Forgiveness is not for the faint of heart. If it was, it would be a lot easier to do! We all know that good things come as a result of hard work. In my opinion, forgiveness, whether giving or receiving it, is at the top of the list as far as hard work is concerned.

Step 4 Accept and embrace your need to be forgiven first. After this, you will be able to forgive others more readily.

HE WHO LAUGHS, LASTS!

Now that I have turned on the tap to my creative juices, I realize it will be hard to contain all I have to say in just thirteen chapters. I have chosen the number thirteen to coincide with the subtitle of a baker's dozen. I already see the makings of another book. It's hard to believe that twenty-five years ago I could not finish the first chapter, and now the tap is running so fast and fierce that I can hardly keep up.

Over the last several years, my husband and I have had a neat arrangement. He usually is not a man of many words. I am a morning person, and he is not. When we walk in the morning, he says very little. On many occasions he has told me to just keep talking and says that he will let me know when he doesn't agree with me. So he must be agreeing with me in most instances because he usually just keeps moving along in silence. According to Wilma Askinas, "Sometimes you have to be silent in order to be heard."[20] Publius Syrus recommends, however, to "let a fool hold his tongue and he will pass for a sage."[21] Either way you look at it, I must admit that I already know what he does or doesn't agree with. If I want to get him to talk, I just press one of his buttons, but most of the time I hear his silence and know exactly what it means.

All kidding aside, I prefer to see him as the sage

that I know him to be. This really does work for us, but sometimes I feel that my neck is a little further out on the limb than his is, seeing as I'm the one doing most of the talking while he's just walking! This actually coincides with one of his famous sayings, "walk the talk." He much prefers to live what he believes rather than talk about it. He feels that actions speak for themselves. I agree because it's a lot harder to actually do something than it is to talk about it. Our preference is to live in a do as I do world rather than a do as I say one. The former builds relationships on a foundation of credibility, which results in more mutual respect and admiration. At times, however, we actually walk in silence, each with our own thoughts.

I must admit, although, that despite his silent personality, he is the king of the one liners. He may be a man of few words, but when he uses his now famous lines, he's a riot. If there is anyone who can get people to laugh, it is him. Just the other day when we were sitting on our back deck with some of our family, he literally had us in stitches. The grandchildren know about my book writing endeavors, and I told them that maybe one day I would write a book about their grandpa and his ability to make people laugh. I suggested to one of them that she go get a piece of paper and write down all his funny quips. We literally laughed for well over an hour in the backyard while enjoying a sunny afternoon outdoors. The more we talked and laughed, the more the ideas flowed. Almost every time we mentioned an occasion where Grandpa had made us laugh, it triggered a memory to another equally funny occasion. Our children and grandchildren had a hard time leaving and only did so because they had another engagement. It was a pleasure to see their reluctance to leave, but the laughter enjoyed by us all that afternoon will not be soon forgotten.

Although our grandchildren would love to see a book totally devoted to their grandpa and how funny they think he is, they will have to settle on a chapter for now.

The type of afternoon I mentioned in the previous paragraph was by no means the first time that we've had a good laugh at Grandpa's expense, nor will it be the last. In fact, he enjoyed it so much he kept coming up with even more funny one liners. Our young granddaughter could hardly write fast enough to jot them all down. Ever since that day, we have seen our grandchildren several times, and each time that Grandpa comes up with one of his sayings, they quickly run to write it down. Of course you realize that I probably would need a book to share them all with you, so I will try to pick out a few to tickle your funny bone. I hope you get a laugh out of them, not unlike the rest of our family. This is written to honor my husband as the father of our children and as grandfather to theirs. I know it will be well received because he will know that it comes from the spirit of love that his family has for him. After all, "a little nonsense now and then is relished by the wisest men."[22] I truly believe he is one of those men!

When I asked the girls to try and think of some of Grandpa's funny sayings, the first one blurted out was, "It's hard to soar like an eagle when you are surrounded with turkeys."[23] It reminded me of an earlier time when I asked my husband to help me stuff the turkey at Christmas.

Full-time working mothers can use a little help in the kitchen now and then, and I was no different. My husband has always referred to himself as an "eater, not a cooker." He has absolutely no interest in preparing any kind of meal. If he has the occasion to be home alone, everyone knows he will have toast for his meal, no matter what time of the day it is. Actually, he will have toast and peanut butter because that is his all-time favorite meal. He can also prepare himself a cup of tea because he does know how to boil water.

At this particular Christmas celebration, I was quite busy with all the preparations. After I mixed the stuffing, I asked my husband if he would stuff the turkey while I went on to prepare other things. I showed him the turkey cavity where the stuffing went. This was a new experience for him as he never even realized that turkeys have such cavities. I then went about my other business. Big mistake! When

I eventually looked his way, he had gotten the meat tenderizer out of the drawer and was using it like a hammer to literally pound the stuffing into the turkey with all his might. He was stuffing that turkey like there was no tomorrow.

With a smile on my face and a twinkle in my eye, I asked him what the heck he was doing. He answered by saying that he was simply following my instructions. To him, stuff meant to pack down firmly, and he had done a fine job of doing just that. I could hardly get the stuffing out of the turkey to serve for supper. As far as I was concerned, there seemed to be more than one turkey in the room, one doing the stuffing and the other being stuffed. I'm thinking that maybe my husband was the eagle after all. I never asked him to help stuff the turkey again, and I'm not so sure that this wasn't his goal in the first place. We had a good laugh over this episode.

Subsequently, this reminded me of a similar episode. Before we got married and I was still living at home, on Sundays or for special celebrations, my dad always carved the meat at suppertime. He really enjoyed this little task, and I loved it as well, because if I hung around, he would always give me a few small pieces of meat to eat. These morsels always tasted so good before supper, because I was especially hungry. I liked this tradition so much that I tried to incorporate it into our family life after we got married.

When my husband said that he was an "eater, not a cooker," he really meant it. It was another one of those family celebratory occasions, and once again I asked my husband to give me a hand. I had prepared a roast of beef, and I wanted him to carve it for supper while I strained the gravy and mashed the potatoes.

I really should be more specific with my instructions. While I was otherwise occupied, my husband counted the number of people present, took the electric knife in his hand, and proceeded to carve the roast into the number of chunks that we needed to correspond to the head count of who would be dining with us. It's a good thing the pieces were so thick. If anyone wanted a second helping, there were none to be had.

No more roast carving, no more turkey stuffing; this husband of mine knew exactly what he was doing. A person may not always appear to be the sharpest knife in the drawer, but my husband was honing his skills at staying out of the kitchen in such a laughable way. Although I was on to him, I continued to go along with his antics. When I repeat some of these stories, he will turn to the grandchildren and say, "I don't like Grandma's attitude."

This comment about my attitude triggered another funny memory. Before mon epoux (my husband) retired from his chosen profession, he had many people who had reported to him over the years. He had also been a very busy man in other ways with on the job traveling and all the other demands that went with his position. Therefore, he had neither the desire nor the opportunity to spend a lot of time in the kitchen. After he retired, however, he had plenty of time to spend in the kitchen, and he chose to do so. He had absolutely no interest in taking up any kind of cooking, which I would have happily turned over to him without a moment's hesitation. He was not interested in this particular position because he preferred his old one of being an "eater, not a cooker." I, on the other hand, had spent a great deal of my time in the kitchen, not only planning and preparing meals but loading and emptying the dishwasher as well.

Now, because of his surplus of time, my husband decided he would become an efficiency expert. Even though I had held this kitchen job for well over thirty years, upon retirement, my husband decided that I did not know how to properly load the dishwasher. He proceeded to try to teach me how to do it in a better, more efficient way. Needless to say, I did not think that I needed to be taught how to do this task because, obviously, I had more experience in the kitchen than he did.

Once again, with a smile on my face and with a twinkle in my eye, I explained to him that just because so many people had reported to him in the years before he retired, I didn't need him to be the boss of me now that he had retired. He turned around with an expression to match my own and said that he was going to report me to human resources because I had such a bad attitude. How can you not laugh at a comment like that? Kind of takes the wind out of your sails. He probably reported me to the grandchildren.

I needed to share these stories with you so that you could better understand the importance of sharing your life with someone who is so in step with you and the way you view the world. My husband is one of those guys. He shares my pleasures and my sorrows, but of the utmost importance, he also shares my sense of humor. According to Ann Landers, "A good laugh is the best lubricant for oiling the machinery of human relations."[24] It is with my husband that I have learned how to laugh and enjoy life to the fullest. His sense of humor has enhanced mine and has been the oil that has kept our relationship blooming.

We can usually find the bright side to just about anything. This has been our saving grace in facing the ups and downs of daily living. It has been said that "it is worth a thousand pounds a year to have the habit of looking on the bright side of things."[25] So in other words, it is probably where some of our greatest wealth lies because in most instances, this is how we choose to view life. "Choose" is the key word here and the one that should be remembered.

Many years ago, before our retirement when we were in the throes of raising our then teenagers, my husband and I were already trying to look on the bright side of things, and he was already busy trying to find ways to make us laugh. My husband even went so far as to photocopy a sign, which he gave to our daughters. It read:

> *"Teenagers...If you are tired of being hassled by unreasonable parents, now is the time for action! Leave home and pay your own way while you still know everything."*[26]

Then if one of them would be too busy with her teenage life, he would say to her, "Sometimes you act as if you're not even my child." He has a line stored in that mind of his to meet all occasions.

It's ironic that not much has changed in that respect even to this day. Now our grandchildren have taken over and are finding many ways to amuse us. After a small scolding, one of my granddaughters, at four years old, with her hands on her hips, said to me, "Grandma, you've been mean to me twenty-nine times." When I turned and smiled at my husband, she wagged her finger at him and said, "And I mean you too, Grandpa!" There was also a time when my grandson, who was an early talker, said to my husband while driving, "Two hands on the wheel, Grandpa!" We get such a kick out of all they have to say and continue to develop our sense of humor to this day.

Grandpa also has a grand time playing cards with our grandchildren in much the same way he used to play with their mothers. Two of the most enjoyable card games they played are Old Maid and Go Fish. Unknown to our daughters when they were young, after playing the game of Go Fish for long periods of time, he would eventually get tired and want the game to come to an end. In order to do this, he would then start to pretend he had the required pairs of cards needed to bring the game to an end. In some circles this would be called cheating, but who is going to find fault with a dad for playing cards with his children for hours on end? Not me, that's for sure! For years, our daughters could never quite figure out why the cards in their hands never matched up, but somehow their dad's cards always did.

When he finally admitted to them what he had been doing all those years, one of our daughters never forgot that story. She later shared it with her children. One day when we were playing Go Fish with our young granddaughters, the oldest one, who was eight years old at the time, said to her five-year-old sister, "I'll sit beside Grandpa because he cheats." At last, we got a good laugh on Grandpa. He was speechless!

We try to find as many things to laugh about as possible in our own realm because in the outside world there is often times little to laugh about. We only have the power within our own sphere of influence, and this is where we choose to use our time together in as much laughter as we can. We have experienced much sadness, and we have made every effort to enjoy the good times and appreciate them.

I have one more story I would like to share with you, which exemplifies both our desire and ability to do this. Like most families these days, my husband and I are a two car couple. The two vehicles we own are a four door car, which I drive most of the time, and a Jeep, which my husband usually drives. When I do little errands with my mom, I always take the car because it is easier for her. One day, both my husband and I were going to pick her up to take her shopping. My husband went into the garage ahead of me and got in the driver's side of the car. After setting the alarm, I got in the passenger side of the Jeep because when we go out together, my husband always drives the Jeep. My husband was watching me the whole time and never said a word or made a sound. So there I was, sitting in the Jeep, and when I looked over at him, he was sitting in the car splitting a gut. Now you know why I not only have but need such a sense of humor! It is called survival.

I have had what seems to be a lifetime of this kind of bantering. Between my husband and my daughters, I have had absolutely no choice but to find humor in everyday occurrences. I actually cracked up myself because I looked so ridiculous sitting in the other vehicle. We both got such a good laugh out of such a simple thing. Over the years, we have learned to laugh at ourselves and laugh with each other. My husband has taught me how to really laugh, the kind of laughter that you feel at the back of your throat, all the way into your chest. It's the kind of laughter that causes tears to run down your cheeks and turns people's heads. It's the kind that heals your woes and cleanses your soul. It's just so neat because it is in these moments when you really get each other. This is the kind of laughter that enhances your life and all your relationships!

What Pritchard has to say further proves my point, "You don't stop laughing because you are old: you grow old because you stop laughing."[27] So on that note, do everything in your power to develop your sense of humor and find someone to share it with. "Make happy those who are near and those who are far will come."[28] Happier people are more fun to be around and usually spend their time with like minded individuals.

I realize that life has many serious moments, but I also know that it is necessary to have a well developed sense of humor to deal with most of what life has to offer. We need to take the time to have a really good look at our lives and all the positives in them. It's better to learn to laugh at all our little mistakes and the mistakes of those around us. Try to keep joy in your life as much as possible. Look for the small things in life that bring you pleasure and happiness and seek to increase them. After a while, the small things will add up. When you keep things simple, you don't need a big event to keep you happy, rather a smaller, more attainable series of joyful occasions to sustain you. Be grateful for the small pleasures in your life, and more will come your way until your life is very pleasing to you.

An older friend of mine who has since passed away said to me that the kingdom of God starts on earth. C.S. Lewis confirms this by saying, "Aim at heaven and you will get earth thrown in. Aim at earth and you get neither."[29] If this is true, and I do believe it is, then it is time to enjoy some of those pleasures in the here and now. The way to do so is to find happiness in everyday events. Remember, it depends on how you choose to look at life and all that it has to offer that brings you everlasting joy! It is much wiser to dwell on the good things in our lives because "the longer we dwell on our misfortunes, the greater is their power to harm us."[30]

Find things to both smile and laugh about with your lifetime partner, your children, your family, and your friends. "Laughter is the shortest distance between two people."[31] Work at narrowing the gaps between you and the people in your life with the appropriate use of humor, and so many relationships in your life will be healed. We really do need to laugh more.

I must admit that I was going to write a totally different chapter here instead of this one. The other is yet to come. I decided to veer off in another direction for now. I thought that it was time to lighten up a bit and see another side of life that is near and dear to my heart. It has been said that "We give of ourselves when we give the gift of words: encouragement, inspiration, guidance."[32] I hope that in some small way the simple examples of the laughter my husband and I have shared will be of guidance to you.

Step 5 Laughter really is the best medicine. Take it in high doses when necessary!

YET ANOTHER F WORD!

N ow I am going to write the chapter I intended to write before I veered off in the other direction as mentioned in the last chapter. I told you that it was yet to come, and here it is. I always try my best to be true to my word, and I am delivering as promised. I am going to start with a bit of humor here to get my point across. In my life, I have heard the expression over and over again, "I'll never forget the time when..." Usually when I either say or hear these words, it is in reference to some memorable or funny event. I truly relish most of these memories, and I am so appreciative that my mind has such good recall. However, I do notice that at times I have a few blips when I can't remember someone's name as easily as I once did. My husband reassures me it is because we now have so much information stored in our memory banks that it takes a little more time to sort through it. I hope he's right. I can well imagine what it must be like for the elderly and how frustrating this can be. I'm pretty sure that you have now figured out what the F word I am now about to discuss is, but just in case you haven't, it's the word "forget."

A lot of my favorite "I'll never forget" stories revolve around occurrences in the past that have to do with my children, my grandchildren, my parents, and my in-laws, as well as extended family and friends. I'll never forget how my oldest granddaughter, who is now twelve, started to write me little notes on the clipboard in the bathroom when she visited. We have a little habit in our house of keeping the latest crossword puzzle on a clipboard in the washroom. These notes from my granddaughter have long since progressed to a notepad under the bathroom sink. Every time she visits, my granddaughter takes a rather lengthy bathroom break and writes me a note. After she goes home, I go read the note and write her back, putting the notepad back where I found it.

At the beginning, she used to print her thanks for the good supper or for having her and her sister over for whatever reason. Now she is into writing instead of printing, and while the notes are still full of thanks and appreciation, we write about other things too. We never verbally discuss this habit with each other. We just keep communicating in this enjoyable and rewarding way. I sure do hope I never forget this shared joy, and I sure hope that she doesn't either. As the notepads fill up, I have even retrieved them from the garbage after she tosses them out because I do believe one day they will bring her even greater pleasure. I have saved them in my night table along with all my other cherished mementos.

Another one of my unforgettable stories involves my oldest grandson. After raising three wonderful daughters and then being further blessed with the birth of two beautiful granddaughters, along came the first boy in the family. I must say he's quite the gifted talker. He does not miss a thing. One time, when he was about the age of two, my daughter had picked me up to go shopping. As we were driving along in traffic, the motorist beside us accidentally ran over a squirrel. Due to the fact that my grandson was so young, my daughter did not want him to be traumatized by this incident, so she motioned to me not to say anything. She wanted me to just keep looking ahead as if it hadn't happened. All of a sudden we heard this small voice from the backseat asking, "Why'd that guy run over that beaver?" As I'm writing this story, it still puts a smile on my face and joy in my heart. Why would I ever want to forget such a cute occasion?

Another unforgettable memory occurred not too long ago when babysitting my four year old granddaughter and her younger brother. The time had come for him to have his nap. My granddaughter looked at me with those big blue eyes of hers and said that her brother needed mimis to fall asleep. She wanted to know why mine didn't have any milk. I told her that they only have milk when you have a baby and that her mommy was my baby. Oh, if only you could have seen the smile on her face and the look in her eyes while she digested this information as things registered. No one would ever want to forget such a precious moment.

I did manage to get my grandson to sleep without the mimis. However, I tried at least three times to lay him down after he fell asleep, and each time he woke up and cried. Finally I gave up the idea of putting him down and just sat on a chair in our bedroom. He slept on me for one and a half hours. I never want to forget how precious he felt to me as I held him in my arms and how grateful I was that he was sleeping so comfortably.

In the last chapter, I referred to other unforgettable moments and how they have brought me such great pleasure, especially the "You've been mean to me twenty-nine times, Grandma" instance. There are so many things I never want to forget, and I hope I never do, especially when it comes to my grandchildren.

Now I am going to get into the more serious side of this chapter. I can't count the number of times that I have heard or read about the need to forgive and forget. I used to find these words of advice quite troubling. I really felt that there were many times that I had forgiven a slight or a transgression, but for the life of me, I just couldn't seem to erase it completely from my memory bank. If I recalled it, it made me second guess myself into thinking that perhaps I hadn't really forgiven the person who had offended me after all. It took me a long time to realize that maybe I wasn't supposed to forget, or maybe it was merely impossible for me to do so.

Some of the things I remember may be unhappy

events or circumstances; however, most of them are not. You can't completely turn off one tap without turning off the other. There is absolutely nothing wrong with admitting that someone may have offended you by their actions. It is both totally appropriate to remember that you were hurt and also possible to know that you have forgiven the person at the same time. Memory is memory. In time, bad ones do fade, but if you repress bad ones and refuse to acknowledge your feelings, it only makes for difficult times later on in life. "Let us not look back in anger, nor forward in fear, but around in awareness."[33]

Actually, it has started to make more sense to me that we aren't supposed to forget, at least not completely. We need to remember so we can prevent similar occurrences and the repeating of similar offensive behavior, whether on the receiving end or the giving end. "We make progress if, and only if, we are prepared to learn from our mistakes."[34] This is not about grudge holding, but more about learning from past experiences and/or mistakes. Forgive the person, but make every effort to not forget the lesson. Forgive yourself too, if the hurt feelings had to do with your own inappropriate behavior toward someone else. By all means, however, register the lesson learned and store it for future reference. We wouldn't get too far in life if we just kept repeating history.

I read a book some time ago, called Cry Anger by Jack Birnbaum, M.D. I actually got angrier while

I was reading it because it put the onus of what was going on in my life smack dab at the base of my own feet. It states that "people get angry because they try to hide how they are feeling and they push it deep within themselves."[35] It goes on to elaborate about being compulsively nice and being afraid to show what you really feel. When you do this you have a tendency to keep repeating the same cycles of behavior in your life. Before you know it, you take on the not so desirable victim status. You need to truly learn how to break the bad habits of such destructive behavior. In order to do this, you need to remember what people or what actions led to these bad past experiences. It is the only way that "you can prevent illness, improve your self-image, and learn to enjoy life,"[36] according to Birnbaum.

So once again I reiterate, forgive yourself or the person/people involved, but try your best to not forget the lesson. Remember too that life is full of lessons, and there really is a lot to learn. I do think, however, that the old cliché of "an ounce of prevention is worth a pound of cure" really holds true here. Once you adopt this habit, when you have more positive experiences, good memories will replace bad ones.

I can't tell you how happy I was when I came across an article written in USA Today that confirmed some of this philosophy. It was titled, "Forgive Doesn't Mean Forget" by Cathy Lynn Grossman. It's a story about the Amish community being lauded by clergy for showing forgiveness to the killer of five little girls whom he had murdered. I have felt quite far out on the limb with this belief of mine about forgiving but not totally forgetting, and I was grateful to discover that someone else agreed with it. It's about forgiving the person in spite of the action. It is about learning to differentiate between the two. You can still love the person but not what they did. "Forgiveness doesn't mean condoning,"[37] says Kula, author of Yearnings: Embracing the Sacred Messiness of Life. He feels that forgiving allows us to continue on our personal journey. Therefore, it is possible to forgive the person but still not condone the unacceptable act by that person.

This is why I feel that we need to look at what caused the breakdown in our own personal relationships to begin with and then do some soul searching to prevent future similar occurrences. When you truly forgive, the memory of the betrayal will not be in a toxic place because it will be stored in the proper place of learning from past experiences.

I also read another article that stated that just because you have forgiven someone doesn't mean to say that you have to be friends again. With this thought in mind, however, you must remember that "no love, no friendship can cross the path of our destiny without leaving some mark on it forever."[38] This is refreshing to me because the friendship that you may once have shared with someone has given you both the opportunity to learn and to also see something positive in a relationship that may no longer exist. It takes time and work to eventually come to this conclusion.

Sometimes, people are no longer compatible for whatever reason. In my opinion, it is better to admit it. It is always best to act on your upset feelings because "merely ignoring a problem will not make it go away...nor will merely recognizing it."[39] According to Walter Pitkin, "all bitter feelings are avoided, or at least greatly reduced, by prompt-face-to-face discussion."[40] Acknowledging a problematic relationship and making every effort to deal with it is a good step to a healthier self. If an open and honest discussion does not resolve the situation, then you must decide on a different course of action. We already know how hard it is to change ourselves, so is it really wise to expect other people to change to suit us and our own needs?

If discussing the problem doesn't work and the bad behavior does not stop, the best advice that I can give you is to move on. Try to glean the good that was once in the relationship or the lesson you learned from it. It is much easier to choose to have people in our lives who share our belief systems and values. Therefore, I repeat that it is possible to forgive and not forget as long as you continue to learn from the experience. It may very well mean you will not be friends with someone you once considered a friend, but once you have forgiven them, you can still be friendly or civil toward them. This is part of the healing circle. I'm taking Patrick Henry's advice here when he says, "I have but one lamp by which my feet are guided, and that is the lamp of experience."[41]

In conclusion, I want to say that some topics are so closely related that it is best not to separate the two. It is better to expound on the philosophy when the opportunity arises in order to tie up more than one loose end. All the points I have made thus far are the kind that link together in a very intimate way. To try to completely separate them in a standalone fashion would make them separate suggestions, giving them less of an impact. As stated in my introduction, the first four steps are vital to the healing process. There is much overlap between all four. They act as a cohesive group of problem solving points and are more closely related than others. Some of the topics for my suggestions are more serious than others. The first four definitely fit into the more serious category.

This sixth step ties in very closely with the chapter on forgiving and being forgiven. As stated earlier, it may be impossible to totally forget instances that have caused you so much grief. The goal is to try to learn from these experiences and to try to replace them with memories of happier times. After a while, when the negative cycle is broken, those memories that you actually want to forget will go further back into your memory bank. They will be replaced by new and positive experiences that you don't want to forget.

Step 6 Cherish your memories, but use them wisely. File the negative ones, but remember the lesson learned.

WHO'S ON FIRST?

As I was walking the other day and thinking about this chapter, it brought me so much joy. For those of you in my age bracket, you probably know the comedians Abbott and Costello and Laurel and Hardy, as well as Lucille Ball. I was raised in an era of slapstick comedy that some of the younger generation doesn't always get. I must admit, though, that some of the things they find funny I don't always get either. Perhaps some of you have seen the baseball skit by Abbott and Costello. It involves a lot of verbal confusion about who is on what base, as well as a lot of laughter surrounding the confusion. The reason that I am referring to this funny little skit is that sometimes in life we get confused, just like these comedians. Who's on first in our relationships can be a very challenging decision, but, unlike the skit, it is not very amusing at times.

This chapter is very important to me because it is on intimacy and marriage. The relationship I want to dwell on is marriage, although any long term relationship may benefit from my findings. Marriage is a word to describe a lifelong commitment. There are many people who can relate to this chapter of life. Simone Signoret says it better, in that "it is threads, hundreds of tiny threads, which sew people together through the years. That's what makes a marriage last—more than passion or sex."[42] I believe that life's joint experiences are the threads that bind couples together in the most intimate way.

My husband is asleep as I pound away at the computer in my slow, rhythmic way. I took a typing class in eleventh grade and really haven't typed much since. In that class all those years ago, I had the unforgettable opportunity to meet my husband of thirty-eight years. Even then, he was the strong silent type. It didn't take me long to notice him and his good looks. He thinks I'm teasing when I tell him that I told one of my girlfriends how I had my eye on him. He says it was the other way around. So we continue to tease each other by saying that "he ran after me until I caught him." And what a fine catch he has been!

I remember my dad advising me in those younger years. Even at sixteen years of age, in my most rebellious stage, I took his advice. I married a man with the same kind of faith and the same kind of background as my own. So, I must agree with Ovid when he says, "If you should marry suitably, marry your equal."[43]

I do believe I did just that, but it does not mean to say that we have not experienced the ups and downs of life within that marriage. It's what people experience within a marriage that binds them together in a unique and memorable way. It wouldn't be living if our lives were void of the trials and tribulations that life has to offer. "Seldom or never does a marriage develop into an individual relationship smoothly and without crisis. There is no birth of consciousness without pain."[44] Our marriage has not been unique in the sense that we have been exempt from life's perils.

If our marriage stands out in any regard, it would be because of the honesty and love that we have enjoyed within it. Thoreau is right when he says that "between them whom there is hearty truth, there is love."[45] My husband has two of my favorite qualities. He is an honest man with faith. "Honesty is not only the first step toward greatness, it is greatness itself."[46] It has also been said that "honesty is the indispensable essential of every worthwhile success."[47] In those first few years of our relationship, even before we got married, he was a young man with those same characteristics. He has remained an honest man and maintained his faith, not only in God but in me as well.

In order for a marriage to be deemed a success, it too must have a solid foundation based on honesty. Honesty in a marriage consists of your spouse wanting to know all about you and fully accepting who you really are. In my introduction I explained why my husband used to ask me what I was jongling about. My husband wanted to be part of my innermost self. He wanted to better understand me and for our relationship to be more open. He realized that all my jongling was a sign that I was troubled about something, and he wanted to know what it was so he could better support me. He wanted me to be more open and honest with him, and I was able to tell him what I was jongling about because I trusted him. When he asked me this question, I knew that he wanted an honest answer, and I gave it to him.

Long before this time, my husband had known my thoughts on pretty well everything. Putting pen to paper is only actually giving these honest thoughts a longer life span. I must say that my husband has also shared his views with me about these thoughts. Rest assured, if he didn't agree with what I was thinking, he never hesitated to tell me. My opinion of his thoughts or philosophies has the same wide stroke. If I disagree with something he says, I say so.

In an honest relationship, you don't have to agree with everything that is being said or done. The most pertinent part about the honest relationship is that it is not threatened by the fact that you may not agree. At times, I have used the expression that I have to do what is right by me and according to my own conscience. I expect my husband to do the same.

I discovered very early in our courtship that he was the man I wanted to marry. He was the one whom I wanted to be the father of my children and whom I wanted to spend the rest of my life with. I can honestly say that I feel the same way today that I did all those years ago, and I have absolutely no doubt that my husband shares this sentiment. The security of this feeling has only made me want to try harder to be worthy of it.

If I had to pick another characteristic that sustained and enhanced our marriage over the years, aside from our love for each other, it would be the fact that neither one of us ever tried to change the other. When looking around at some of the troubled relationships that have unfolded before us, I would have to say that the main reason for the breakdown of those marriages is the desire to change the other person. I am not perfect, my husband is not perfect, but because of our deep devotion to each other, we have always just chosen to accept one another.

"A good marriage is that in which each appoints the other guardian of his solitude."[48] Each of us has the undeniable right to be ourselves and to cherish our own uniqueness. Although my husband and I have both matured with time, I would have to say that we have actually become more of what we were first attracted to, not less. Even today, if my husband does something to irk me, I remind myself that I knew what he was like before I married him. For instance, how could I possibly complain that he is the strong silent type today, when it is this quality that made him attractive to me in the first place? If anyone gets married with the intention of changing the person after the wedding, the marriage is headed for disaster. Remember, if you love someone enough to marry them, you are agreeing to marry them as they are, not what you hope to change them into after the wedding. It doesn't mean to say that you can't see the potential for all that they can become, but you must respect who they are in the here and now.

The staying power of a lifelong relationship also includes the need for loyalty. It is impossible to have an honest relationship without loyalty. If my husband displeases me or vice versa, the first and only rule of thumb that we have ever used and still use is to discuss our displeasure with each other. We don't draw other people, including our own children, into any of our disagreements. In fact, there are many people who might think that we have never disagreed, but that would be virtually impossible. We merely choose to be loyal to each other and not air our differences in public.

Over the years, I have heard so many people criticize their spouses when they weren't around. It's almost like a form of male/female bashing. When men or women put down their partners in one way or another, how can you have a mutually respectful relationship? It's impossible. It's always amazed me that when the spouse walked back into the room, it was as if nothing had been said. I could never quite figure out how you could say negative things and turn around and be so lovey-dovey with the person you had just criticized. It never made sense to me, and that's why I chose to never engage in this type of behavior. I simply could not see the point of it, nor could I see any benefits. If anyone tried to put down my husband in any way, I would refuse to hear of it. I would defend him to the nth degree. No one has ever had my permission to come to me and find fault with my husband nor will they. If they have a problem with something he may have said or done, they have every right to approach him about the situation.

I call this trait loyalty because I see loyalty as the desire and conviction to stick by and with your mate through thick and thin. My husband offers me this same consideration. To my knowledge, no one has ever come to him and found fault with me either. It's just the way it is. It doesn't mean to say that we don't have spirited conversations with our family and friends, it only means to say that we do not talk about each other in a negative way to anyone else.

Without ever discussing it, at the very onset of our relationship, we somehow mutually agreed to this philosophy. I cannot tell you the pleasure and the feelings of security that this concept has brought both of us over the years. Neither one of us would ever put our upset feelings over the love or loyalty we feel toward each other. It is during these times when we fully realize who's on first. It is learning to rise above our displeasure without compromising our values. The only way to correct the situation is to talk to the person, not about the person. This takes maturity and self-control. Talking about the problem with someone else never solves it, it only perpetuates it. First and foremost, you need to discuss the problem with your spouse.

I must admit that my husband has always been somewhat ahead of his time. It has been of great benefit to me that he has always considered me to be his equal. I never truly realized the importance of this concept in our earlier years. As a matter of fact, I'm not so sure I even recognized what it was until later on in life. We started off as friends in that eleventh grade class all those years ago and have remained friends to this day. Confucius said, "Have no friends not equal to yourself,"[49] and no truer words can be spoken.

This is an excellent rule to adhere to because it can only enhance a friendship. In fact, I would go one step further and say that if you consider someone to be less than yourself, the relationship that you have doesn't even fit into the friendship category. Treating each other as equals certainly added to our friendship and subsequent marriage. This applies to all relationships, not just marriages. God made humans with their ears at the side of their heads for a reason. It is so that they could walk side by side with their partner or their friends on an equal footing.

There are no lesser human beings in this world. We are all equal, one no more or less than the other. I realize that life has evolved over time, and women have fought for equality in all walks of life. To have found equality in a role that would not necessarily be deemed successful by society has been very rewarding to me and to our marriage.

Not too long ago, we were sharing a wonderful evening with some of our friends down south. After supper, our host did a unique thing. As we sat around the table, he asked each of us to share something about ourselves and something about our spouse. My husband's turn was before mine due to the seating arrangements. He said something that was music to my ears. He told these friends of ours that he could never have been the success that he was without all my support and coaching over the years. He gave me equal credit for our success, although my role would have appeared secondary to a lot of people. I, too, give him full credit for the support and coaching he gave me in my role as wife and mother. Although I did work outside the home throughout our marriage, my main role was homemaker.

We never differentiated between the importance or the value of either role. We saw the crossing over into each other's lives as the threads that strengthened our bond as husband and wife, which resulted in a secure environment for our children. It was shared responsibility and success on both fronts. We never felt alone in important decision making times. We always utilized each other's skill or expertise in order to make the best decision for us all and for the home we were providing for our family.

Both of us realized very early on that we had our weaknesses. In retrospect, it seems that his strengths were my weaknesses and vice versa. We needed each other in order to be better at what we were doing and what we could become, whether inside or outside the home. We chose to tap into each other's resources rather than go it alone in our own realms. Neither one of us wanted the full responsibility of making all the decisions in our own area. It is this sharing of information, responsibilities, and ideas in our lives that has kept out marriage so vibrant. It has been both mentally challenging and personally rewarding to be involved in all decisions that affected us as a family. A good marriage is grounded on a mutually respectful relationship based on the good judgment and trust of your spouse.

Love in marriage is vital for its survival, but sometimes the meaning of the word is elusive. Perhaps instead of calling this chapter "Who's on First," I should have called it "What's on First." If and only if you go into a marriage accepting the person as they are, wrapped in the old fashioned values of honesty, loyalty, and equality, will you find the secret of a happy, lifelong relationship. La Rochefoucald said it best when he wrote, "no disguise can long conceal love where it exists or long feign where it is lacking."[50] Love is nothing but a meaningless word unless it entails the stated qualities as mentioned above.

When you realize what is important, you will never be confused like Abbott and Costello about "Who's on First." It will all fall into place. "It makes all the difference in the world whether we put truth in the first place, or the second place."[51] Take the time to reflect and define what love really is to you. Start with this truth! After that, if you truly choose to love, the rest will come easier. When you love someone, you show it by cherishing and respecting them. In order to expect love, you must be willing to offer it, "for it is not fair to ask of others what you are not willing to do yourself."[52]

Step 7 If true love is what's on first, there will be little or no confusion in your marriage as to who's on first.

SILENCE IS A
DOUBLE-EDGED SWORD

Well, it happened, and I knew it would eventually. As I begin writing this chapter, I don't even have a title for it. The original title and chapter I wrote were both a bust. After I finished writing the first one, I wasn't completely comfortable with the results. I almost alerted my husband to this fact; however, I didn't want to take the chance of swaying him just in case it was better than I thought. Although I never told him of my own reservations, my suspicion was confirmed when I gave him the chapter to read. Instead of coming to tell me what he thought about it, he busied himself in some other way. Not a good sign!

It reminded me of the white rice that I served him for the first few years of our marriage before he got the nerve to tell me he didn't like white rice. In those days, I didn't have the insight to notice how much he was or wasn't eating because I was so busy enjoying what I had prepared. I was the cook, and I loved rice, any kind of rice. So needless to say, we ate plenty of it. It brings a smile to my face as I remember his hesitation in wanting to tell me he disliked rice while at the same time making every effort to spare my feelings. It was déjà vu all over again. It reconfirmed my view about how powerful silence can be.

A few days ago, one of my daughters used that same strategy. There was no feedback to the chapter I had given her to read! Yuck! So now we all know the strategy of how this is going to work.

As powerful as words might be, when you are expecting verbal feedback and it doesn't come, the silence is extremely loud and meaningful. I cannot believe the impact that both of these silences have had on me. My daughter eventually expressed what was bothering her in a roundabout way. By probing my husband for his opinion, I was eventually able to draw out what I needed to know. I reassured my husband that I was thicker skinned than he thought and that I valued his input. I know that "a thick skin is a gift from God,"[53] but I also know I got a little cheated in this department. It's not to say that I'm unhappy with my other gifts, but I do recognize my shortcomings. Getting my husband's opinion goes a lot further than this. I not only value his opinion when it comes to the writing of this book, I need to know that I can count on his good judgment just in case mine is off. So this is where the truth in our relationship really needs to pay off.

Although my feelings count, I want to make sure that everyone else's do too. "From error to error, one discovers the entire truth."[54] I may be the cook of this book, but we both have to be comfortable with the results. I want to make doubly sure I do it right. You just never know in life how far something will go or how successful it will be. This could become bigger than my wildest dreams because "fortune sides with him who dares."[55] Therefore, this has to be a book that we are both comfortable with and prepared to stand by just in case we are fortunate enough for it to be a hit. So I do indeed want to take him and all of his feedback into consideration. I hope that Eleanor Roosevelt is right when she says that "a woman is like a tea bag: you never know how strong she is until she gets in hot water."[56] I have a sneaking suspicion the same holds true for a man. You really do need two tea bags to make a good pot of tea. I'm quite happy to have him in the hot water with me. There is no way he's bailing out now.

When I get up in the morning, the first thing that I do is put on the coffee pot and the CD player. I sit in my rocking chair, enjoy my cup of coffee, and listen to the softest music. It is during this time of solitude that I am most inspired to write this book. This is my quiet time because my husband likes to sleep in, and I am a very early riser. I offer him the same kind of quiet time except that his is at night instead of the morning. I go to bed early, and he gets to enjoy his space in the evening. We are very respectful of the other's need for space, especially now that we are both retired. I find at times, though, that I am almost stretched between the desire to listen to my music and write this book. As the ideas flow, I do not want to miss the opportunity to write them down for fear of forgetting them later. "The thoughts that come unsought, and, as it were, drop into the mind, are commonly the most valuable of any we have."[57] So I am making every effort to combine the two pleasures and enjoy them both.

As stated in an earlier chapter, my husband and I started going out at a very young age. Due to our youth, we dated for close to four years and got married when we were twenty years old. During this courtship phase, I had the opportunity to spend at lot of time with my future in-laws. They were very generous in sharing their Sunday meal with me. I was very eager to get to know them better and spend this time with my then boyfriend.

Although I enjoyed his whole family, my future father-in-law was the one who really intrigued me. He was the exact opposite of my father. I know I have referred to my husband as a silent man, but I have never met a more silent person than his father. Sunday after Sunday, we would share this delicious meal and then play cards. We all would laugh and enjoy the card game, yet he seldom said a word. When I would visit, he would usually tease me by saying, "Are you here to eat all my food again?" I would look at him and see the twinkle in his eyes, and mine would twinkle back. Sometimes when I arrived I would ask him if he missed me, and he would answer by saying, "Where were you?" I would just smile. Once again, I would see the twinkle in his eyes, and once again mine twinkled back. This went on for years.

I can honestly say that we never had one real discussion or even what you would consider to be a decent conversation during all the years that I knew him; however, I felt such a love and warmth emanating from this dear man that I can still feel it to this day. His silence never blurred the love that he was able to show by the expressions on his face. No words could have ever taken the place for what I saw in his eyes. It was a true paternal love for his children, and he included me as one of them.

At nineteen years old, my husband and I became engaged, and we got married less than a year later. At the ripe old age of twenty, we considered ourselves ready for marriage. My husband was a full-time student at the time, and I worked full time to support us for the first couple of years. He was able to contribute to our financial situation by working on construction during the summer.

Due to our own innocence and little forethought, by the age of twenty-two, we had our first child. When she was less that a year old, in order for my husband to pursue his education, he accepted a position at an accounting firm about an hour and a half from where we lived. We decided that it was best to just move to this small city and make it our home so my husband could devote his time to articling in the accounting firm while working full time as well as finishing his education. I found another teaching job and a babysitter for our baby daughter, and life went on.

After a couple of years, much to our great pleasure, I discovered we were going to have a second child. I continued to teach until the end of the school year. I was about eight months pregnant by then. During the summer, my husband would go back to university full time and stay with his parents. I stayed home with our two-year-old daughter so that he could concentrate on his studies. He came home every weekend. On the day that I went into labor, I discovered that we were having twins. We were overjoyed with this wonderful news. Little did we know the fatigue that was about to follow.

After two days of labor and a few days of recuperation, I was sent home with two four-pound baby girls. My mother spent two weeks with us to help out, but after that, we were on our own. I was so grateful to my mother for her help because I agree with Bertha Von Suttner when she says that, "after the verb 'to love', 'to help' is the most beautiful verb in the world."[58] I cannot tell you how tiring that first year was for both my husband and myself. We were like two zombies dealing with two babies and a two-year-old toddler. If anyone needed help at that time, it was us.

About six weeks after the twins were born, a dear friend of my mother-in-law decided that because we had unexpected twins, she would host a shower for us. Although we were very tired, we drove into the city to attend the shower. Everyone wanted to see the twins. It was our first trip back to the city since their birth. After the shower was over, my husband's family, along with us, gathered at his childhood home. It was September, and we started to talk about Christmas being just around the corner. Due to our circumstances and our fatigue, I explained that it would be so much easier for us if they all just came to our house, and we would make the Christmas meal. My sister-in-law was a few years younger and still single. My brother-in-law and his family were much more mobile. He was eight years older than us, so his children weren't babies.

After discussing this situation for several minutes, my sister-in-law made a comment. She simply blurted out, "Well, then, Merry Christmas!"

Internally I took it to mean that if we couldn't be there for Christmas, it was no big deal. She had no idea what we were experiencing because she was at such a different stage in her life, although she was only a few years younger. It wouldn't surprise me if she didn't even remember the occasion, yet I remember it so vividly, and so does my husband.

As tired as I was, I had no idea how to respond. I just looked at my husband and said, "I think we better leave before I say something I regret." There was dead silence in the room as we packed up the babies. We never discussed it again. My husband and I got into the car, and we didn't discuss it with each other either. We didn't have the energy or desire to say another word. We just drove home in silence. I have no idea what was said by the rest of the family after we left. They never mentioned it again.

On Christmas Eve, we drove into the city with our young family. Much to our sadness, my father-in-law was unwell and never got out of bed except to go to the washroom. At one such moment, he turned his head and looked my way. There was such a sadness and weariness in his eyes that matched my own.

My brother-in-law and his wife ended up hosting Christmas. It was the first time that we didn't spend Christmas in the traditional way. I'm sad to say that we never had another Christmas meal around that family table again, where we had eaten and played cards so many times before. Less than three months later, my father-in-law passed away. Oftentimes, I have wondered what that silent father thought of this whole situation.

We have had many happy Christmas celebrations since then, but for me and probably for my husband as well, despite all the joy we have known, there is always a hint of sadness at this time of the year. It is not only because pepere never saw another Christmas. It is mostly because he never got to know our children and now theirs. He missed so much. It is equally sad that they never got to know their sensitive, loving, and teasing grandfather. They would have absolutely loved each other. I know because I can still see his face and the twinkle in his eyes.

Silence is an extremely powerful tool. It has been almost thirty-five years since my father-in-law died. His silent personality has stuck in my mind all these years. He could say all he needed to say with so few words. When I recall that last Christmas together when he didn't get out of bed, I can't help but ask myself if he was making a silent statement of sorts. Seeing him the way I did, I have a feeling he may not have been comfortable with what happened.

I have used this strategy myself. If I feel too emotional about a situation, I remove myself from it in order to better cope. The silence that came after this family episode was deafening. Not hearing from anyone nor having any further discussion about what had transpired meant a firm no to our request. Although we left before I could verbally say something I would probably one day regret, our leaving silently said it all. We all said so much with silence that day.

The one comment that I wish had remained silent was the one made by my sister-in-law. This is an example of when silence could be golden. She never meant any harm. She was coming from a place of innocence and ignorance. She had no idea about the responsibilities that go with working full time, going to university, and raising a family, all at the same time. My husband and I were much too tired and stressed out to see her comment in an unemotional way. "Reason only controls individuals after emotion and impulse have lost their impetus."[59] I did not want to hurt or offend anyone, and in the end, my silence may have not been golden either because it might have caused so much grief for my dear father-in-law who meant so much to me. Silence...it can cut either way!

Words or lack of words can carry some pretty strong messages. The silence of my husband and my daughter in the first example held a powerful message. The silence of my father-in-law with his twinkling eyes that carried so much love also held a powerful message. The silence after my sister-in-law's comment was deafening. The silence that ensued after that was equally deafening.

Silence can be both positive and negative. Sometimes you need to talk to get a message across, and other times you don't. In retrospect, I think it would have been better if we had talked about it again at a later date. I don't think we all should have remained so silent. Silence is okay sometimes, but we could have utilized much better communication skills in this instance. Even after all these years, I still wish we had! I've come to realize over the years that if a situation arises that you aren't comfortable with or that you don't agree with, silence is a form of acquiescence. In other words, you can tacitly agree to something by saying nothing.

Step 8 Silence really can be golden, but not always. Lack of words can be as powerful as the use of words and very effective in getting your message across. Just keep in mind that words can be likened to swords. They can cut to the quick if we speak before we think.

MAKING MONEY TAKES
COMMON CENTS

Money...yes, this chapter is about money. Is it the root of all evil like it has been said? I think not! Over the years, I have discovered that first and foremost, money needs to be respected. It can cause so much joy or so much pain. Having too much money is not necessarily a good thing. Too little money can also be negative, especially if you can't meet your basic needs. Even if you have plenty of money, the way you choose to spend it can have a variety of positive and negative effects on both yourself and those around you.

Some people love having money more than actually spending it. They care more about the amassing of it in order to feel wealthy or financially secure as they watch their bank account grow. This is how they get their pleasure. Others can't spend it fast enough, sometimes spending it before it is even earned. Some of these people live in a world of credit cards and heavy debt load. Those who live like this care a lot about purchasing things and can often times be caught up in the philosophy of consumerism that exists in our society today, the one of "buy now, pay later," which is much more popular than it was in my youth. I'm sure that Artemus Ward was jesting when he said, "Let us all be happy and live within our means even if we have to borrow the money to do it with."[60] This statement is what I call a true oxymoron! I must admit that although in my era we did use credit cards, it wasn't quite with the same marketing encouragement and vigor that they are used today.

The peer pressure to keep up with your friends and neighbors is far greater than it has ever been. It seems that when it comes to advertising, everything you read or watch on television points to buy more and the sooner the better. This advertising also stresses that you will be happier if you do just that. We live in a new and improved era where bigger and better are the main themes. If you can't afford it, just charge it. As a matter a fact, almost every store will offer you the credit you need to buy everything you actually don't need!

This is quite the sales marketing strategy, and it is definitely not a good thing. It really does work, however, because it fits in with what most people crave—not having to wait for anything. In fact, it is so easy to just go buy whatever your heart might desire that you would look foolish to try to save up for something that you could have right now. My goodness, no one would want to look that foolish! If everyone else is doing it, why would anyone think otherwise? That is the million dollar question and the one that begs to be answered.

I have lots of these so called old-fashioned views, but when it comes to money, I see the misuse of it as one of the major causes of marital problems and conflicts today. It is one thing to not have enough of it, but the greater disservice to a spouse and children is the lack of responsible spending when you do. So many marriages break down because the couple cannot agree on how to properly spend the income that they have. Often times the income is adequate, but the priorities are different between the husband and wife on how it should be spent.

If one partner believes in buying on credit all of the time without any regard to a repayment plan, there will be nothing but trouble ahead. Once you start to overuse credit cards and are unable to pay the bill in full each month, you end up paying interest on interest due to the fact that interest rates are so high. Before you know it, your credit card is maxed out! Not to worry, though, because the credit card company will gladly raise your limit so you can keep doing the same thing over and over again.

Guess why. This is how they make their money. If you do this with several cards, before you know it, you will be in a fine fix. Not only that, the "buy now, pay later" philosophy will only end up making you pay more for an item than the original cost. Half the time, you may still be paying for an item that you no longer even possess. I'd certainly sooner do without a few things than get myself in this kind of bind. What never ceases to amaze me, however, is the willingness of so many people to do just that. Saving up to buy something makes a lot more sense to me. According to George Macdonald, "To have what we want is riches, but to be able to do without is power."[61] I agree wholeheartedly with this statement. If you have the discipline to say no to yourself and your desire for things, in the end you have the greatest power over your own financial destiny.

I once read that it is not how much you have that gives you true wealth but rather what you can live without. The only truly effective way to use credit cards is to use discipline when making purchases. When using credit cards, it is a good habit to pay them off in their entirety at the end of each month. If you are unable to do this, you are better off not using credit cards at all and just learning to live within your means. I would like to say that if you have common sense and a lot of discipline, credit cards are good in an emergency. The difficult thing is to define what an emergency really is to both you and your family.

One of the reasons that I have labeled this chapter "Making Money Takes Common Cents" is because, as indicated in the previous paragraph, people really need to make their money work for them, not against them. The only way this can be done is for it to be a joint effort. Unless you have some kind of great wealth where money is not an issue, the "my money, his money" philosophy just doesn't work in most good marriages.

I think that most major disagreements in a

marriage are a result of poor money management and different spending priorities. I strongly recommend that spending habits be addressed before a marriage. I do believe it is a vital part of marriage preparation. If your partner has bad spending habits, as I referred to in "Who's on First," he/she will not be changing this habit, or any other ones for that matter, after the wedding. In fact, if that expectation is there, it will only result in resentment.

Try to make sure you know what habits are really important to you. It may be all right to disagree on minor things, but money isn't one of them. One of the most difficult couple combinations is where a frugal person is married to an extravagant, "live for today" type of personality. There is untold grief ahead for such a couple, as one tries to make ends meet and the other keeps moving the ends as a result of his/her spending sprees. There will be plenty of frustration and resentment in this relationship, especially if there are children involved and some of their needs are being sacrificed by irresponsible spending habits.

"Responsibility walks hand and hand with capacity and power."[62] Making your money work for you means working together using common sense and embracing your powers of personal discipline. Common sense usually means combining your resources into one household income so that "the right hand knows what the left hand is doing" and everyone's needs are being met. When you get married, most people usually decide to do this unless they have agreed to something else up front.

Working together to meet your needs can only be accomplished by being on the same track or wavelength. It's up to the couple to decide just what track that will be. If both people within the relationship, however, are big spenders living with the "buy now, pay later" philosophy, I can guarantee you that reckless spending catches up to pretty much everyone. The only way that it won't is if there is some bottomless pit when it comes to the amount of money you have to spend. Most couples don't start off this way, and a lot of couples don't even end up this way.

Now I am going to use a really old-fashioned word to describe good money management skills. That word is "budget." I'm talking here about trying to live below your yearnings. Please excuse my play on words, but I just couldn't help myself. I'm talking about living within your means. In many cases, the only way to do this is to make a budget of your income and expenses and go from there. If you really can't afford some extra item because it doesn't fit into your budget, then you just don't buy it. I know you may have a hard time wrapping your mind around this idea, but I can assure you it is the only one that works if you don't want to get caught up in the spending "rat race." Once you make up your mind to use this strategy, it will start to come much easier, for "doing is the great thing. For if, resolutely, people do what is right, in time they come to like doing it."[63]

This good habit of living within your means can be very rewarding indeed. Remember again that good habits are as hard to break as bad ones. Remember also that we live in a world filled with capitalism and consumerism. It is very hard to resist getting caught up in the attractiveness of this world and the temptation to want everything in it, even when we can't afford it. Last, but not least, remember that "the greatest blessing of our democracy is freedom. But in the last analysis, our only freedom is the freedom to discipline ourselves."[64] Each and every one of us has the power within to do this, regardless of what anyone else might think about it. In "Listen Up Some More!" I encouraged you to dare to be different. Responsible spending would be a good place to start!

Step 9 In a good marriage/relationship, the wisest thing to do is to combine all of your resources. Using common sense in all of your decision making, including financial matters, will only enhance your life and your future together. Common cents makes common sense!

THE HEAD IN THE BOX

Before I address the true theme of this chapter, I want to explain that I have changed my strategy of sharing each chapter with my family as they are written. I do believe that initially this was a good idea, but after writing the first half of the book, I started to realize that I was giving my family more power than I was comfortable with, in so far as their reaction to it. Although I needed to know what they thought of my writing capabilities at the beginning, I soon realized that my creative juices weren't flowing as freely because their feedback had become overly important to me. I have now informed them that they will all get to read the final chapters when the book is completed.

Although constructive criticism can have its value, it can also backfire in the sense that you can start looking for approval rather than being the free spirit that we are all intended to be when we are exercising our creative abilities. Criticism and advice go hand and hand. According to Samuel Coleridge, "Advice is like snow: The softer it falls, the longer it dwells upon and the deeper it sinks into the mind."[65] Giving and receiving criticism is an art that is not easily developed. The wisest course of action is to be miserly with the giving of it so as to have the greatest impact and acceptance on the receiving end of it.

My husband's belief in me and in the writing of this book before he knows what I am about to write is my inspiration to finish what I have started. He has the ability to see the unseen, and he has encouraged me to forge ahead with its completion. This thought actually ties into the theme of this chapter, which I am about to share with you.

Last winter when we were down south, we had the pleasure of visits from two of our daughters and their children. During these visits, we had the opportunity to do many more things than we would normally do, but in spite of all the activity, we still did some of our routine things. In the evening when it was time to relax before bed, we watched television most nights as usual. One of our favorite shows is Law and Order, and during the visit with our older grandchildren, they got to watch it too. If you are a fan of the show, you know it always starts with the crime scene at the beginning and with the solving of the case following this introduction.

In one particular episode, after the initial crime, when the detectives got back to headquarters, a square box was delivered to the department. As they were in the process of opening the box, I said what I was thinking out loud. "There's a head in the box!" Before you know it, there were cries of disgust as the detectives discovered that there was indeed a severed head in the box. My eleven year old granddaughter looked over at me and asked, "Grandma, how did you know that there was a head in the box?"

I glanced over at my husband, who also knew what was in the box, and we both tried to explain to our granddaughter how we knew. We then discussed the voice of experience with her. What was so apparent to us was not at all apparent to her at her young age. It seems that often times when we watch these crime shows, it feels like we have seen them before, even at the beginning of a new season. So ever since that show, my husband and I have come to use the expression of the "head in the box" to explain a lot of what we have been observing or how we feel about a particular set of behaviors. It has almost become our own little method, mode, or actual code of communication.

Every time we now see something that happens that is so predictable or obvious to us, we refer to this. We have come to realize that our granddaughter is not the only one who doesn't always have the ability to see into the future, or in other words, have the ability to predict outcomes. There are all kinds of clichés to describe this "gift," such as "reading between the lines," "reading the writing on the wall" or "seeing the unseen." I am using the term loosely in referring to it as a "gift" because it is actually a skill or a discipline that usually becomes better developed with age and experience.

I must add, however, that not everyone has the

desire or ability to acquire this skill. The combination of the two is necessary for it to become a more effective tool to better live our daily lives. We reassured our granddaughter that as she got older, she too will have better mastered this technique. The question she asked us that night kind of gave us a picture to some of life's frustrations and to what probably causes the majority of us a lot of problems. It creates in us an expectation of behavior in both ourselves and in others that can lead to both positive and negatives experiences or disappointments. "Discipline does not mean suppression or control, nor is it adjustment to a pattern or ideology. It means a mind that sees "what is" and learns from "what was."[66]

Many years ago as a young student, we had many lessons on the why, where, what, who, and how of things. I specifically recall these lessons as early as third grade. I also remember how much I disliked this subject matter. It was very difficult to digest all the information in reading comprehension and to develop analytical thinking at such a young age. It did not come easy for me. I considered it to be one of my tougher courses, which did not bring me much pleasure at the time.

I must admit though, as the years have gone by, I am very grateful to have had those lessons, as difficult as they may have been. I realize that in those days there was a lot of stress on the three "Rs" of education, those of "Reading, 'Riting and 'Rithmetic," but I also know that it did have its benefits. Education today is so profound and in many ways over my head with all the computer technology and various teaching techniques that have come about. I do believe, however, that it is essential to effective living to have the ability to analyze a situation and to be able to predict the outcome of human behavior in as many situations as possible. It is necessary to have this skill in order to shape our lives in a more positive and rewarding way and in doing so help shape the lives of those around us.

I have called this a skill or a "gift," but perhaps the best word to use to describe this ability is "wisdom." Some people refer to it as the "gift of wisdom," but I personally know that it is not a "gift" that is easily attainable or always well received. I prefer to see it as a "gift" that is achieved. "It requires wisdom to understand wisdom: the music is nothing if the audience is deaf."[67]

If you have experienced any hardship in life, you usually acquire some wisdom along the way. If you don't learn from past experiences, life can be very painful and frustrating. It is also quite frustrating to witness those around you who are unwilling to hear what you may have to say that could help prevent undesirable occurrences or suffering in their lives.

There are many well-educated people, people who are book smart, but these same people are not always adept in making wise life choices. There is a huge difference between education and wisdom. Sandra Carey says it best in stating that "never mistake knowledge for wisdom, one helps you make a living: the other helps you make a life."[68] You actually need the knack of the "head in the box" theory, to put it mildly, in order to better your own life. Not all people realize the importance of this ability, but life would be much easier to endure if we all strove to achieve a least some level of mastering it.

The benefits of wisdom are not always highly regarded or appreciated by others who are not aware of its attributes. It is a slippery slope, to say the least, to learn when to advise and when to bite one's tongue when it comes to the use of this "gift." There have been times that if one were to take me literally in this sense that my tongue would have been bleeding profusely as I said to myself, "mum's the word." It actually gives new meaning to the word "mom." I may know what I know, but I try my best to choose my words wisely before I speak. In spite of all my forethought, I must admit that I am not always successful. It is very difficult to not eschew a few words of wisdom as the need arises.

I must continually remind myself that words of wisdom are also seen as words of criticism. There is such a fine line between the two that depending on how you view it, sometimes these words can be seen as similar to the "great divide." If these pearls of wisdom are not received the way they were intended, it is very difficult to feel otherwise.

Therefore, I am fast coming to the conclusion that you need even more wisdom in order to effectively utilize the little bit that you may have acquired along the way. This is one of life's many conundrums. It's a bit of a poser as far as I'm concerned and one that I have not completely figured out thus far. It reminds me of my earlier school teaching years in the primary grades when listening to the children read aloud. I cannot recall the number of times when I just wanted to say the word that the young student was trying so desperately to sound out. I cannot help but be amused at the restraint that we must all learn in life in order to not blurt out the answers.

It takes plenty of self-discipline as we try to sit by and let our children and their children figure things out in their own way and in their own time. Oh yes, to be a mom is also to be a teacher. The true test is learning when to be a mom and when to be mum. Believe me when I say that this is one of the real challenges in the raising of a family. I've also noticed that it is a major challenge in all of our relationships. No one, and I mean no one, wants to be told what to do, or in other words, wants to have the benefit of someone else's experience or knowledge, no matter how good our intentions may be.

I will tell you a cute little story that proves my point. We have been going out on a regular basis with one particular couple for supper over the years. We thoroughly enjoy their company and have frequented several restaurants together. We go out for supper with many other couples as well, but often times on shorter notice, my husband and I do enjoy dining alone.

We like to try different meals in different restaurants. After some trials and errors, we usually figure out what we like, what we consider worth ordering again, and where we most like to eat. My husband had ordered a particular meal in one of our favorite restaurants, a meal that did not leave a lasting impression on him once when we dined out alone. Sometimes, he will even go so far as to ask me to remind him not to order a particular meal again because he has a greater tendency to forget such things.

When dining out with the previously mentioned couple, my husband was about to order this very meal. I indicated to him that it wasn't one of his more enjoyable meals, so he just ordered something else. I must admit, though, that I was quite amused by the other couple because they both ordered that very meal the next time we went out. I couldn't help but smile to myself when they did this. I observed that neither one of them was overly impressed with the meal itself. We have been out with them several times since at that very same restaurant, and not unlike my husband, they have never ordered it again.

This, to me, is just a small example in a very innocent type of situation that proves people like to make their own decisions and draw their own conclusions. If it is our human nature to be reticent in taking the advice of people even in the simplest matters, we cannot expect to be any more receptive when it comes to more serious ones. Obviously, it does not get easier with age. I do believe that the older we become, the more resistant we are to listening to others as well. So as you can see, this causes yet another conundrum, that of not being open to advice at any age.

Therefore, whether you can predict that there is a "head in the box" or not, no one really wants you to blurt it out, and everyone pretty well wants to claim that they already knew it was there. Also, most people who cannot predict it was there prefer to bury their heads in the sand and go about their business in their own ignorant way. Needless to say, I'm pretty sure that's why the saying of "ignorance is bliss" still flourishes today.

I fully agree with Ernest Hemingway's philosophy, which states that he likes listening and that he has learned a great deal from listening carefully. He goes on to say that most people never listen. I could not agree with him more; however, I will go an extra step. The less we listen, the more we trip up. The more we trip up, the more we learn. The more we learn, the less we will trip up in the future. So either way, we will eventually learn our lessons in life, whether by the hard way or the easy way.

I truly believe it is a personal choice, and it is our own to make. "No man is great enough or wise enough for any of us to surrender our destiny to. The only way in which anyone can lead us is to restore to us the belief in our own guidance."[69] Failure really is success turned inside out. According to Wendell Phillips, "What is defeat; nothing but education; nothing but the first step to something better."[70] It just depends on how you look at life and life's experiences.

What I am basically trying to say is that most of us attain wisdom by learning from life's lessons. Aristotle concurs when he says, "What we have to learn to do, we learn by doing."[71] Most of us want to share the benefit of these lessons with those around us whom we love. We would like nothing better than to spare them the suffering that we have endured in learning these same lessons. It would seem, however, that in most cases, those around us prefer to live their own lives and learn their own lessons.

In the end, wisdom is experienced only by walking in the footsteps that lead to it. It is something that is attainable only by living life to the fullest. It cannot be taught like other subjects. All the knowledge or reading in the world cannot produce it. It comes from within, and when you find it, you are ever so grateful for the simplicity of this precious "gift." At times, you actually chastise yourself for not recognizing and appreciating it sooner. In actuality, it is one of the few "gifts" in life that you earn. It would be similar to having the respect of other people, in so far as to say that this too is earned.

My husband continues to tease me, as I have the tendency to share my philosophy on what life is all about. He jests when saying that he can't figure out if I'm a know-it-all or all-knowing. I finally have the answer for him! I'm a know-it-all, because I've discovered "it's what you learn after you know it all that counts."[72]

Step 10 Cherish your ability to predict the "head in the box." Learn how, where, and when to share some of the insight that comes with this ability. Learn how to appreciate life's challenges in doing so.

FACT, FAIRYTALE, OR FICTION

Just when you may have thought that my sense of humor had gone south, here I am with three more "F" words, which I am about to build on in this chapter. I know that some of the previous chapters are more serious than others, but I do like to lighten up on most subjects as much as possible. It's not to say that I don't take life seriously; it's only to say that I try not to overcomplicate most things if I can help it. According to Ceran, "Genius is the ability to reduce the complicated to the simple."[73] I am still making every effort to hone this skill, and in order to do this, I will invariably use some kind of story to get my point across. I have not only chosen to do this in book form, because those who are closest to me know that I am forever the storyteller verbally as well. It is usually my chosen way to best get my point across. I must admit I use it frequently. It has served me well over the years because it has been an effective teaching tool on both the receiving and giving ends.

It would seem that I best learn from the stories I have heard. I usually try my best to glean whatever message is in them that may apply to me in order to better enhance my own life. More often than not, regardless if the story is based on fact or fiction, there is a moral to most of what is being read or written.

This also holds true for fairytale type stories, which most of us don't read anymore, unless we have young children in our lives.

When I was teaching primary school all those years ago, not unlike the children, I used to enjoy the little stories in the readers that we used at that time. Not all, but a lot had a moral to them. The children always loved these stories too. They were not only easy to read, but they captured their interest as well. Most students were keen on knowing how the story ended. These were the kinds of stories where I asked a lot of open-ended questions afterward that provoked thought, moral development, and values in these young students.

I once heard from a seasoned teacher that the majority of children have formed most of their basic personalities by the age of six. She was not talking about academics, but about morals and values. One of the primary ways that most children have learned this is through the use of books read to them by their parents or caregivers. At this early stage of life, pretty well all the direction that children receive has been in the form of fairytales or cartoons when it comes to developing life skills. I am not talking about the "don't touch, that's hot" kind of direction but rather about the kind that there is good and bad in this world. Young children are taught very early in life that they can't trust everyone. This is done very subtly with the use of childhood books. Some of these examples are found in the familiar and simple fairytales of The Three Little Pigs, Little Red Riding Hood, Cinderella, Sleeping Beauty, Snow White, and the list goes on. Several of these stories have become movies or cartoons which give a visual, animated picture. I would think that this has been done to try to educate a child as early as possible to be careful around certain kinds of people.

Other values are taught as well, such as being kind and considerate to others. It doesn't take long for children to realize whom they would like to be in the stories that are being read to them, and it is usually not the bad guy. When I have read some of these very stories to my own grandchildren, they have said to me, I don't like that guy. They have even gone so far as to point to the ogre in the story while shaking their heads in a negative way in order to stress their dislike before they could actually verbalize it.

As adults, we have a tendency to forget these basic stories and at times lose sight of some the little lessons taught in these books. I once received a gift when I was in my forties, which was an adult reader that stated that all you ever needed to know, you actually learned in kindergarten. It was a cute paperback book that took less than an hour to read and was full of the kindergarten rules to survival. Surprisingly enough, if, as adults, we were to incorporate the simplicity of these rules in our adult daily lives, there would be a lot more consideration for others and a lot less frustration.

One such similar story that brought both the students and me such pleasure in my earlier teaching years is the one about the little princess who refused to eat. The fact that this young princess refused to eat was of great concern to her father, the king. After the king exhausted the expertise of all his most talented advisors in the kingdom, no one could come up with the remedy to get the princess to eat. The king was beside himself with worry over the dilemma, and as a very last resort, he finally asked the court jester if he could come up with the solution to what had now become a very serious problem.

The reason for this problem was that the king had told his little princess he would give her anything in the world that she wanted because of his great love for her. She decided that she wanted the moon. When he could not provide it for her, she refused to eat because he was not being true to his word. All the king's men could not come up with the answer on how to provide her with the moon that had been promised.

The king found that the court jester, in his simplicity and after years of observation in the kingdom, knew exactly what to do. First of all, he asked the little princess what the moon meant to her. She quickly ran to the window and pointed to the moon in the evening sky. Then he asked her how big she thought the moon was. She quickly put her finger up before her eyes so that she could no longer see it through the window. So, according to her, it was about the size of the tip of one of her fingers. He then asked her what she would do with the moon if she had it, just like her father, the king, had promised. She eagerly said that she would wear it on a chain around her neck.

So the court jester had a necklace made for her that carried the moon. He put it around her neck, and the princess was so pleased that she started to eat again, much to the relief of the king. Then the king asked the court jester how he would explain it to the little princess when the moon was in the sky on the following night.

The jester found the explanation to this question by simply asking the little princess for the answer. He started by asking her what happened when one of her own teeth fell out. She quickly answered that another one grew back in. So that was the very explanation the court jester gave her for the new moon in the sky.

Such a simple story, I must admit, brought so much pleasure to those young minds so many years ago. Now for the moral of the story, which is still so relevant today. There is actually more than one. In fact, I'm sure there are some that I may have overlooked. To me, the one that stands out the most is the reluctance of the king to ask the opinion of the least educated man in the kingdom. He failed to realize that "the quality of a person's life is in direct proportion to their commitment to excellence, regardless of their chosen field of endeavour."[74] It was only as a last resort, after he had gone to all his greatest advisors, that he looked to him for any advice. He could not see the true worth of this man because he did not think he had any worthwhile credentials. He did not think he was smart enough to have the answer, so he had judged him on face value rather than looking at him in the same regard as his valued advisors.

The court jester knew exactly what to do because he could relate to the little princess and could figure out exactly what she meant. He was wise to remember that "seeing through is rarely seeing into."[75] He had the ability to effectively communicate with her and see what she wanted from her angle.

The second moral of the story is just that, figuring out better ways to communicate. Wow...isn't that a skill that we could all use to this day? How many of us struggle with communication skills, and how many of us have lesser regard for others who have what we perceive to be lesser status in life?

Just look at this simple little fairytale and all it has to teach. I must remind you that although this is just a fairytale, there's plenty of fact in it to better educate ourselves. Even in this fairytale, it just goes to show, "It isn't how much you know, but what you get done that the world rewards and remembers."[76] I'm sure that the court jester gained some respect after he came up with the solution to this problem. Perhaps the king learned his lesson in realizing that the next time he was in need of practical advice, he should not assume that wisdom has nothing to offer. As Syrus said, "Many receive advice, only the wise profit from it."[77] Hopefully, we all have the insight to recognize it when it is being offered.

Wisdom and education work best hand and hand. Although I have mentioned the two morals that I see in this fairytale, I will be dwelling on the first one. The theme of my next chapter has to do with effective communication, and I will elaborate more on that subject when I write it.

When I think about the king in this story, it brings to mind our hierarchal society and how we have a tendency to want to move on up in the world. People with more education, higher job positions, bigger houses, wealth, and so on seem to be more highly regarded by society. There may be cultures that I am unaware of that do not see things this way; however, it has been my experience that this rule of thumb generally holds true in most instances.

As I have stated in "Silence is a Double-Edged Sword" about both my husband's and my humble beginnings, another story comes to mind about my father-in-law. This is a story based on fact. He worked all his life to support his family on quite a scant wage. In his early sixties, he was laid off from his job and was visibly upset because he would not be receiving his old-age pension until he was sixty-five. There was quite a gap that he needed to financially bridge.

Needless to say, it was not going to be easy to find a job. He managed to snag one at a big manufacturing company as the janitor with the help of one of his sons. Shortly after he started his employment, there was an annual Christmas party that was being held for all the employees and their families. My husband and I were married at the time, although we did not have any children yet. My husband's brother was also married with two children, and his sister was single but no longer living at home.

My father-in-law was quite happy to have the pleasure of inviting us all to this family Christmas party, in spite of our ages, and we made him proud by going. I will never forget that day as long as I live, for "Put your heart, mind and soul even to your smallest acts. This is the secret of success."[78] My father-in-law showed us around his new place of employment and described his work to us as if he was the president of the company. It has been said that "every job is a self-portrait of the person who did it. Autograph your work with excellence."[79] I was so busy looking at my father-in-law do just that, as I observed the personal pride he took in a job well done, that I'm sure I missed most of the tour.

I learned a very valuable lesson that momentous day, so many years ago, from that very simple man. It's not what you do that counts but how you do it that matters most. The reason this story comes to mind in association with the first one is because our parents, with their lack of formal credentials, would have been at the same level as the court jester in the fairytale story, so to speak. I can certainly tell you, though, that they had plenty to offer as far as teaching morals, values, and the ways of the world to their children. It's not that they knew everything, but what they did know, they did it with pride.

Simply put, they had work ethic. Just observing my father-in-law that day proved it to me. He took such pleasure in sharing what he did to make a living with all of us. Maxim Gorky says it best. "When work is a pleasure, life is a joy! When work is duty, life is slavery."[80] I have seen people in much higher walks of life, according to societal values, who have not known such personal reward for a job well done. Rather than looking at what a person does for a living, perhaps looking at how he does it is of greater value.

The king eventually realized the value of wisdom in the first story. The court jester had the wisdom to look at things in a different way, and he succeeded where others had failed. He enjoyed what he did, and he did it right, regardless of how he was viewed by his peers. So this is the way that my husband and I have been taught to look at the world. This is the same way that we have taught our children. We now have the pleasure of seeing our own grandchildren being raised the same way. We always try to bear in mind that "Most people would succeed in small things if they were not troubled with great ambitions."[81] Personal success may be very different from the image that the world has of it.

What I am trying to stress most in this chapter is that it is wise to utilize all methods of teaching in order to get all the skills that we need to better cope with life. These methods of teaching have been offered to us at a very young age and in some of the simplest forms.

According to Albert Einstein, "Any intelligent fool can make things bigger and more complex. It takes a touch of genius and a lot of courage to move in the opposite direction."[82] Getting back to basics and recollecting some of these earlier teachings can still be an effective coping mechanism today. I agree with Einstein...the simpler, the better. He goes even further by saying, "intellectuals solve problems; geniuses prevent them."[83] So it is really true! An ounce of prevention is worth a pound of cure.

All forms of gathering information, whether by reading, watching movies or television, and so on, are all educational tools. Whether the information we are processing is based on fact, fairytale, or fiction, there invariably is some moral or message that can be gleaned from it. If the information is not pertinent at the time, it will be stored for future reference. It is wise to tap into it whenever necessary. Let us remember all those neat dos and don'ts that we were taught at such an impressionable young age and use them today! I can assure you that most of them still apply.

Take the opportunity to draw from all the knowledge that lives within you. Most of what we need to know in order to survive is at our fingertips. All we need to do is maximize on that wealth of knowledge, no matter how far back it goes or in what form we received it. It makes no difference if it was fact, fairytale, or fiction, as long as we learned the lesson that was being taught.

Step 11 Take the time to read between the lines and glean the moral from life's stories.

A LITTLE BIT OF THIS AND
A LITTLE BIT OF THAT!

The only parent left out of the four that my husband and I have cherished so much over the years is my elderly mother. She is eighty-six years old as I write this book, and if she were to see that I had used the word elderly to describe her, I would be in deep poop, so to speak. She would never even dream of using that word to describe herself. I find it quite comical because as my mother has aged, it seems that when she refers to other people in their seventies and early eighties, she says they are still young. It is apparent to me that seeing as she doesn't refer to herself as elderly, neither is anyone else getting any older. Everyone is young now. I find it neat that she chooses to look at life this way.

As our parents age and eventually pass away, there are many things that we want to remember about them. A lot of times when I prepare different foods, my husband wants me to cook some dishes that he enjoyed when he was a boy that his mother cooked for him and the rest of his family. There are certain foods, too, that only my mother can prepare in a certain way that take me down memory lane back to fond memories of my childhood.

Over the years, it has become a family tradition that some of these special foods mentioned above have come to be associated with seasonal holidays. One such favorite that we usually enjoy at Christmas time is tortiere, or meat pie. It is almost ironic that one of the best-prepared meat pies is cooked up by my mother, who is of Ukrainian descent, while it is an all time French-Canadian favorite. This was one of my father's favorite dishes, and, as my mother describes today, she learned to prefect the recipe over time through trial and error. The meat pies that I am referring to have also become a favorite of the whole family.

Although my mom still continues to bake her pies and share them with the entire family, one day a couple of years ago, our oldest daughter became quite concerned. She said that we needed to make sure that we got her grandma's recipe for these delicious meat pies. I suggested she phone her grandma herself to get it. Well, you probably guessed it! Her grandma said that there was no recipe. She just used a little bit of this and a little bit of that when referring to her spices. She said that all she did was taste the meat portion of the pie as she went along preparing it. When it tasted right, she just filled the pie crusts and then baked them.

My daughter then proceeded to make arrangements to go over to her grandma's house for a couple of years in a row just before Christmas to help her prepare the meat pies. The only way she could learn this secret recipe was to be there with her grandma and see exactly what a little bit of this and that meant. My daughter is now the only family member that actually took the time to learn my mother's famous recipe. I don't even have it myself, nor to my knowledge do any of my siblings, because it has never been written down until now. This recipe has been learned by doing. The only way to learn the recipe is to follow in the footsteps of someone who knows it.

It was important enough for both my mother and my daughter to take the time to teach and learn so that when my mother is no longer with us, we will still be able to enjoy that part of our family tradition. That was a smart move on my daughter's part, and I'm grateful to my mother for taking the time to share her secret with her. I'm quite happy to know where the recipe is, and I'm equally happy to have my daughter bake one of those famous tortieres for us. I can hardly wait for Christmas.

Many years ago, during the first year of our marriage, my husband craved a few of those famous meals that his mother had once prepared for him. Sometimes he would ask me to prepare something that she had cooked, and I had no idea what the dish was, let alone the recipe. One of his all time favorites was what he called galette au patate, which was some kind of potato pizza. I had never heard of it before, although I did have some French background on my father's side.

My husband must have really wanted to feast on this meal, because one day, he decided while I was at work that he would surprise me and prepare it for the two of us for supper. At that time, we were living in the top story of a house that had been turned into a duplex. The stairs to get into our suite ran along the outside of the house, with a small landing at the top. When I drove up after work, my husband was at the top of the landing yelling at me to hurry up. Somehow or other he had locked himself outside with the potatoes boiling away on the stove inside in preparation for our feast of galette au patate.

I need to share with you at this point that as new a cook as I may have been, my husband was even newer. This was going to be his first meal ever to prepare. When I opened the door to get into our suite, I discovered that he had bought a five pound bag of potatoes and had peeled and boiled them all. He was so excited about this upcoming meal. I never said a word as I watched him finish what he had started. I know that I would have plenty more to say today, but you must remember that I was a newlywed at the time.

I did ask him, however, how he knew what to do. All of our parents were still living at the time, and he quickly told me that his mother had given him the recipe. You probably guessed it again! It actually was very basic in that it consisted of mashed potatoes and flour. You were supposed to spread this mixture out in the form of a pizza on a large pan and generously cover it with butter. After that, you would then bake it in the oven until it was crispy.

Well, my husband mashed the potatoes and added a little bit of flour just like his mother told him to do. He also spread it on the pans just like his mother instructed. However, when it came out of the oven, instead of being able to cut it like a pizza, it was so soft we had to eat it with a spoon. Yuck!

Needless to say, my first encounter with this special meal was not so special after all. I must admit, though, that it certainly was memorable. I later asked my mother-in-law what my husband had done wrong. First of all, she had no idea how many potatoes he was cooking, nor did he tell her. They both assumed that somehow or other they were talking about the same amount. Second of all, when she meant a little bit of flour, she meant a least a cup or more, depending on the amount of potatoes you were using. A little bit of flour meant only a couple of tablespoons to my husband.

His mother actually did not have a recipe either, just like my mother with her meat pies. She just knew how the potato dough was supposed to feel because she had made it so many times before, and she knew the exact consistency needed to spread it properly and for it to cook up just right. I never did have the opportunity to taste this meal prepared by my mother-in-law, and I have tried to make it myself a few times since. Maybe if I actually had tasted it, after some years of cooking experience, I could have duplicated the recipe.

One thing I know for sure is that this particular recipe is lost to us forever. I have never heard of anyone else who has made it or even knows of it. My mother-in-law could very well have made it up for the pleasure of her own family. I am grateful, though, that I do have a couple of her other recipes. I even have one in her own handwriting, which I cherish as the true keepsake that it is. "Mothers are indeed, the affectionate and effective teachers of the human race."[84]

I am sure by now that if you are still doing me the honor of reading this little book, you know that there is a moral to this story as well. Yes, when it comes to me, it is not too difficult to see the "head in the box." In other words, you should have been able to predict that this was exactly where I was heading.

Remember in the last chapter that I alluded to the second moral that I saw in the story about the little princess and her refusal to eat. It was about the ability of the court jester to effectively communicate with the little princess. In fact, I do believe that he was the only one who actually attempted to do this. All the King's advisors tried to force her to eat, but no one except the jester tried to understand why she wasn't eating. There is a huge difference between these two concepts. One is just telling another person what to do, while the other is about trying to comprehend where the other person is coming from and making every effort to better understand them. It's about taking the time to explain or really teach by discussing or showing firsthand exactly what you mean.

Just telling someone what to do is never enough, and it is pretty well a useless teaching tool. It is necessary to discuss and to try to get feedback to ensure that you both mean the same thing. If this isn't done, all you end up doing is assuming what you think the other person is saying. Effective communication is reciprocal, even when it comes to something as simple as sharing a recipe.

In order to effectively teach, most good teachers are aware of the old adage of "tell me and I forget, show me and I remember, involve me and I learn." My daughter will always remember how to make those delicious meat pies because my mother not only showed her but had the patience to involve her in the process. One of the most important things in this process is doing so you won't forget what you need to know to repeat it.

I am using recipes as an example here to illustrate how muddled things can actually get, even if you think you are giving clear instructions. Feedback is a necessary component in good communication skills. More effective communication leads to less frustration in life. When people feel understood, they have a tendency to be far more positive and cooperative, just like the little princess from the previous chapter.

By sharing these few stories with you, I am trying to impress upon you the importance that meaning what you say and saying what you mean has in our everyday lives. Sometimes things can be about as clear as mud, like my husband discovered with his first cooking disaster. It doesn't mean to say he didn't learn something from the experience, but it certainly didn't have the outcome he hoped for or expected. This happens to us many times in life because we have not made ourselves as clear as we think. Many times too, people will not speak up and pretend they actually understand what we are saying for fear of looking stupid. We need to reassure others in our effort to better communicate that it's all right to ask questions and encourage them to echo what they think they heard the answer to be. This prevents a lot of frustration down the road. "Mistakes are a fact of life. It is the response to error that counts."[85]

I have chosen to write this book not only to help myself but to share my personal recipe on life-coping skills with my children, their children, my family, my friends, and any or all of you who may have been so gracious to have read this book. According to Benjamin Disraeli, "The best way to become acquainted with a subject is to write a book about it."[86] So many times in life, not unlike that special recipe of my mother-in-law's, something good can slip away because no one took the time to write it down. My daughter was astute enough to get the recipe for those delicious meat pies that we have enjoyed over the years.

I now have only one chapter left in this book. Before I write it, I want to say that it is an extra chapter for the bakers out there. Usually there are only twelve items in a dozen, but a baker's dozen has been known to have thirteen. Not unlike both my husband's mother and my own, my recipe for life consists of a little bit of this and a little bit of that borne from my life experiences.

Usually, when I use all of the ingredients and steps that I have mentioned thus far, I end up with a pretty good product. Sometimes, despite my age, my experience, and my efforts to succeed, I can still fail. It is this failure to succeed all of the time that helps remind me of my humanity and the fact that I am not perfect. "When you make a mistake, don't look back at it long. Take the reason of the thing into your mind and then look forward. Mistakes are lessons of wisdom. The past cannot be changed. The future is yet in your power."[87] It has been a growing experience and continues to be as I learn that it's okay not to be perfect and to be just me. "Failure is only the opportunity to more intelligently begin again."[88]

The purpose of this book is to communicate just

that. It would be perfectly all right to choose the part or parts of my recipe that just suit your own needs. Every good cook is known to adjust recipes to suit his/her own tastes. I encourage you to do so. Trial and error are also good teaching tools. In the end, our recipes may be very close indeed; however, "If there is a way to do it better...find it."[89]

Although I have spent a great deal of time discussing effective communication in this chapter, it is only one facet when it comes to better life coping skills. Once this facet is better honed, it will enable you to be aware of all the ingredients in the recipe. In most recipes, if you miss an ingredient or substitute one for another, the recipe itself will still be okay; however, some cannot be substituted for another because the outcome of the recipe will be a flop. In my opinion, effective communication is one of them. I feel it is essential to the success of the recipe, not unlike the first step, that of learning to love yourself.

What I am trying to stress here is the importance of passing on the most important things in your life to your children, their children, and so on. Perhaps some people think it is monetary or material wealth that is important. I think it is so much more than that. To me, the best legacy for our children is information about our morals, values, and general philosophy on life. What I am trying to accomplish is to effectively communicate this by writing this book. Any possible money that we could will to our children will eventually vanish over time. This book has an unlimited lifespan, providing they decide to keep it and refer to it at their leisure.

So many times I have had the opportunity to go to family reunion celebrations. The immediate family, our parents and our siblings, are easy to know, especially if they are still alive. What we don't know, we can just ask. As we look back at our family tree further down the line, we read names, birth dates, and death dates, and if we are lucky, sometimes we see the odd pictures. We have no way of knowing much about what these family members thought and why. By writing this recipe for our children, I thought it would give them a good opportunity to discuss what we were like with their children. Their children may choose to do the same.

Some of the ideas or steps in this book may very well be universal. Instead of just sharing them with our family members, I decided to share them with those of you who are interested. Both my father-in-law and my mother-in-law passed away many years ago, as well as my father. How I wish that I had some of their personal words down on paper. Once my husband and I have passed on, all the memories that we have would be gone with us, and they would be forever lost. Not now, however, because I have taken the time to jot what I consider to be some of the most important ones.

When I shared the fact that I had written a book with one of my friends, I told her that I felt it was kind of personal. I have a lot of respect for her, and she looked me in the eye and said, "personal is universal." So here you have it. As personal as this book may be, there may very well be something in it for everyone.

Step 12 Hang on to your favorite recipes in life. Make sure to write them down before they slip through your fingers and are no longer available to you. Make sure that they are as clear to others as they are to you and that they are passed on to future generations the way that they were meant to be.

THE ROAD OF LIFE

Sometimes in life you will see a picture or image that puts everything that you are thinking into perspective. One such picture comes to mind as I write this chapter, and it is the one of a particular couple that we have met in the retirement community we enjoy down south. The setting we all enjoy is a gated community that offers pretty well everything that retirees of all ages find both fun and interesting. At times, it feels like we are living in a cocoon because we get to do things much more freely than if we lived in a regular neighborhood. For example, golfers ride up and down the streets to get to the golf courses, which would be unheard of under normal circumstances.

In our community, this particular couple has come to enjoy bike riding. The bike that they have chosen to enhance their pleasure is a tandem bike, which is actually a bike built for two. It has two sets of pedals but only one handlebar for steering both bikers. The reason I have noticed this couple more than some other bike riders is because I have not seen another tandem bike in the area. They stand out, so to speak.

Observing them riding their tandem bike reminded me of another bicycle story that I had read so many years ago. It has been stashed away in my end table drawer along with my other treasures. I am going to share it with you today as I have shared it with other people before you.

Before I tell you the story, I want to say that I wish I knew who wrote it. I have called it a story, while others may choose to call it a poem. The message remains the same either way. I have had this story in my possession for so long that I'm not even sure who gave it to me. I probably have had it in my drawer for the last twenty to twenty-five years. I could try to ask around to find out who gave it to me, but I don't think I would be any further ahead. Right at the bottom of the sheet it states author unknown. It's actually typed on a perforated piece of paper. I can see that it is not the original copy, and over the years, I have photocopied it and given it out to a few people now and then that I felt comfortable sharing it with. Every time I have done this, it has been received with great enthusiasm. The story/poem is called The Road of Life.

> At first, I saw God as my observer,
> my judge,
> keeping track of the things I did wrong,
> so as to know whether I merited heaven
> or hell when I die.
> He was out there sort of like a president.
> I recognized His picture when I saw it,
> but I really didn't know Him.

But later on
when I met Christ,
it seemed as though life was rather like a bike ride,
but it was a tandem bike,
and I noticed that Christ
was in the back helping me pedal.

I don't know just when it was
that He suggested we change places,
but life has not been the same since.

When I had control,
I knew the way.
It was rather boring,
but predictable...
It was the shortest distance between two points.

But when He took the lead,
He knew delightful long cuts,
up mountains,
and through rocky places
at breakneck speeds,
it was all I could do to hang on!
Even though it looked like madness,
He said, "Pedal!"

I worried and was anxious
and asked,
"Where are you taking me?"
He laughed and didn't answer,
and I started to learn to trust.

I forgot my boring life
and entered into the adventure.
And when I'd say, "I'm scared,"
He'd lean back and touch my hand.

He took me to people with gifts that I needed,
gifts of healing,
acceptance
and joy.
They gave me gifts to take on my journey,
my Lord's and mine.

And we were off again.
He said, "Give the gifts away;
they're extra baggage, too much weight."
So I did,
to the people we met,
and I found that in giving I received,
and still our burden was light.

I did not trust Him,
at first,
in control of my life.
I thought He'd wreck it;
but He knows bike secrets,
knows how to make it bend to take sharp corners,
knows how to jump to clear high rocks,
knows how to fly to shorten scary passages.

And I am learning to shut up
and pedal
in the strangest places,

and I'm beginning to enjoy the view
and the cool breeze on my face
with my delightful constant companion, Jesus Christ.

And when I'm sure I just can't do anymore,
He just smiles and says..."Pedal."

Author Unknown[90]

I just can't tell you how much I love this story and what its message has meant to me over the years as I sorted out my own life.

Seeing that couple pedal on their tandem bike in our retirement community is a constant reminder of it today. After twenty-five years, however, I have learned that there is another chapter to the story, at least according to my experience. I learned to trust Jesus in my life, but he also learned to trust me on that tandem bike. "Few things help an individual more than to place responsibility upon him, and let him know that you trust him."[91] In my case, it would seem that Jesus only wanted to steer for a while to give me the direction that I needed. As soon as he knew that I could steer, he was quite happy to let me get back in the driver's seat and be responsible for my own life. He also reminded me that once you know how to ride a bike, you never forget. He just took over steering to teach me so that I could learn from his bike riding skills to later go on and teach others.

Once we accept the need to be taught and have a true desire to learn, we ourselves become teachers.

There are plenty of people out there trying to ride their bikes but who just can't find their balance. They may only need someone for a little while to help perfect their bike riding skills. If this is done properly, they will become proficient bike riders and go on to teach others as well.

The true gift of teaching is getting the students to develop enough confidence in their own ability. It is best to not to be overly dependent on the teacher in order to eventually take the place of the teacher in the lives of others around them. No truly good teachers would want their students to be so dependent on them in such a way that they would constantly be in need of their assistance in order to ride their bikes. The goal of all good teachers is to wean their students from themselves, not unlike the mother bird pushing her baby birds out of the nest to make their own way in the world. "You cannot help men permanently by doing for them what they could and should do for themselves."[92]

In conclusion, I am going to end this chapter with a little sense of humor. Many years before my father passed away, he and my mother had the opportunity to visit one of my sisters in another province. My sister needed their help to baby-sit her two young children while she was having surgery. Her oldest son was just over five years old at the time, and he had a baby brother under a year old.

After my sister got home from the hospital, my

dad was enjoying a visit at the kitchen table with my sister and my nephew. My dad was quite the philosopher, and he was having a lengthy one-sided conversation with his grandson. My dad was retelling this story to me one day at his own kitchen table, and he was getting quite the laugh out of it.

He thought that my nephew was sitting there absorbing all that he had to say, and he was so impressed with him. After several minutes of conversation, all of a sudden, my five year old nephew looked across the kitchen at his mother and asked, "How much longer do I have to listen to this guff?"

My dad, his grandpa, nearly split a gut as he retold this story to me. I know that I have philosophized a lot in this book, just like my dad did that amusing day. You can see that the apple did not fall far from the tree. So I would personally like to thank each and every one of you, whether family, friend, or foe, for listening to or reading my guff. I can assure you that there is more of it where this came from, but that is for another day and another book. I am using the word guff not to diminish the importance of anything I have written but rather to evoke the fond memories I have of my dad and the many conversations we shared at the kitchen table. I loved and honored my father, and sitting across the table from him is one of my fondest memories. I will never forget the mirth in his eyes and pleasure it brought him when he shared this story with me. He helped shaped my personality and always respected me and what I had to say. From a very young age, my dad believed in me and treated me as an equal. I am now going to take J. Lubbock's advice as I make every effort to listen to his sage words. He says that "when we have done our best, we should wait the results in peace."[93] I intend to do just that as I wait to see what direction this book will go in.

Step 13 Learn how to ride your bike, and follow all the bike rules as you have been taught. Remember, bike riding is supposed to be fun, so don't forget to enjoy the ride. When you are adept at riding your own bike, take the time to teach others to ride theirs if you sense that they are willing to learn.

CONCLUSION

"You don't write because you want to say something, you write because you have something to say."[94] F. Scott Fitzgerald

Over twenty-five years ago, when I was at a very low point in my life, the first thing I wanted to do when I got back on my feet was to try and prevent someone else from experiencing what I had gone through. For those of you that have suffered from any kind of depression, there is no need to explain why. For those of you living with a depressed person, there is also no need to explain why. The impact on your life and the lives of those around is beyond words. Initially, I wanted to write my recipe for better life coping skills for anyone who would be prepared to read it. As the years went by and our own children got older, married, and eventually started their own families, the reason for writing the recipe shifted to them. Once I completed the book, it then shifted back to embrace a wider audience, and I ended up where I started off. I decided to return to my original plan and share it with as many people as possible.

Right at the onset, I found that it was very difficult to deal with depression, as there is so little understanding when it comes to the cause of it. I've heard the explanation that there is a genetic predisposition to this condition. I've also heard that some people believe it is caused by external factors or something in the environment that we are exposed to that triggers the episode/episodes. From my own personal experience, I would have to say that it is a combination of the two. Other members of my family have suffered from bouts of depression to varying degrees. Depression has a range of being mild, to moderate, to a more severe form known as a major depression. Some people call this form clinical depression. Many people experience what is considered to be the normal down times in their lives as well as others who suffer from mild to moderate depression. The effects of a major depression usually create a devastation that does not allow you to function within your normal routine. I suffered from the devastation of the latter form because I was unable to continue to work at my teaching career when I was experiencing the depression.

Based on my own personal experience, I discovered that it takes perseverance and dogged determination to rise above the depression and move on. It's not to say that you won't have bouts of depression ever again; however, by finding the tools to better cope, hopefully, it will never be as severe. My first bout was the worst. I was off work for more than a year. I thought I had licked my condition, but six months into my new career, I had another bout. I soon realized that my condition was not unlike the situation after a broken arm. Although I no longer needed a cast, I still had to take a little more care so as not to break it again. In other words, I was okay, but I needed a longer healing process. I was off work for six weeks. The hardest thing for me to do was to deal with my feelings of failure and inadequacy. I forced myself to put aside my pride, and I returned to work. I'll never forget how long the hallway felt as I walked down it the first day on my return. Internally, I wished it was longer. Once I faced everyone for the first time, I knew I was going to be okay.

About ten years ago, I had one more bout with depression, but my recuperation time was even less than the first two. The first time, I fell so hard I could hardly get up. The second time, I had better skills, and I didn't fall as hard and got up quicker. The third time, I didn't fall as hard and bounced back even faster. I just kept getting back on the horse after I fell off! The tools I used have been the recipe I've written about in this book. By utilizing all these steps in my life, I was able to overcome my depression in most instances and lead a full and rewarding life. The writing of this book is an example of the kind of reward I am talking about. I hid my depression from everyone for so long with the exception of my husband that, at times, I felt like an actress. It took some time for me to discover that if you play the part long enough, you cease to be the actress and you become the happy person that you were meant to be.

During my struggles with depression, I heard a little proverb/story that helped me put my situation into perspective. Many of us know the symbol of the cross and what it means. A cross is usually used to denote suffering. When some people are experiencing some difficulty in their lives or a painful situation, they may say that they have a cross to bear.

This little story was about a man who felt that his personal cross was too heavy to bear, so he prayed to God to give him another one. God was more than willing to listen to his prayers. God invited him into the room where all the crosses were stored. God opened the door so that they could both step inside. The man was told to leave his cross beside the door. He could then proceed to choose the one that he would prefer. This man did exactly as he was told. In this room he saw many crosses of varying sizes. There were the crosses bearing the devastation of war, famine, poverty, illness, discrimination, lack of education, and anything and everything that one might consider a cross to be. After an exhaustive search through all these crosses, the man turned around and saw this small cross. He turned to God and said that this was the one that he wanted. God smiled ever so kindly and said, "That is the one that you came in with."

The moral of this little story helped me to deal with my cross. As much as I may have felt that I was suffering during my bouts of depression, I know that there are so many people suffering in this world far greater than I could ever imagine. They may very well like to have the opportunity to trade theirs for mine.

As stated in my introduction, several of the chapters in this book start in an almost journal-like fashion. The reason I have chosen to do this is to demonstrate where I started in my healing process, what I've been through, what I've learned, and where I am today. It's to show how far I've come. All those years ago, I thought I had something to say, but I didn't know quite how to say it or exactly what to say. I just couldn't seem to find the right words. The biggest and most profound step for me, however, was finding the courage to say it and write about it. I never thought this day would come because I was so ashamed of myself and my feelings of failure and inadequacy/inferiority. Today, I am full of joy to have found the inspiration, the strength, and the desire to write so openly about my feelings.

My circle of healing ends here, but in essence, it has created a new beginning, as it is only one link in the gold chain of life. Now that I have found my voice, I want to share it with everyone who will hear/listen to me. I want you to know that you are not alone! Try very hard to embrace this fact, and you will start to heal. Trust me. I know that anything is possible with faith, but it takes time. Be patient and give yourself that time. When you see glimmers of light, you will have new hope, and with new hope, you will find a new and happier life.

"Hope is both the earliest and the most indispensable virtue inherent in the state of being alive. If life is to be sustained hope must remain, even where confidence is wounded, trust impaired."[95] Please try to remember that as small as those steps may be toward this happier life, eventually they will all add up, and you will reach your goal! Try to remember as well that I have shared the steps that worked for me. They changed my life.

The first step was the most important because I had to learn to love myself when I felt so unlovable. The next three steps, which involve better listening skills and learning about the need to forgive or be forgiven, are vital to the healing process. Deciding to be your own friend by looking in the mirror and seeing someone that you can actually like by making some necessary changes to help start you off in the right direction. Learning to laugh and enjoying life are good things and should not be taken lightly!

All good recipes can be adjusted to suit someone else's taste. Some ingredients in certain recipes cannot be substituted for others, while sometimes a substitution will create an even better recipe. This recipe is my own. It is what best worked for me and for those around me. I hope that in some way it will also work for you!

For now, this is all I have to say. Tomorrow is another day, and what will be, will be.

BIBLIOGRAPHY

"Leo Tolstoy quotes." Thinkexist.com. http://thinkexist.com/come/quotes/with/keyword/philosophical/ (Accessed August 2, 2008).

"Sprichwort quotes." Love Sayings–Joachim Home Page. www.genevieve-cory.isom.com/music/love sayings.html (Accessed August 2, 2008).

"Lao-Tzu quotes." Thinkexist.com. http://thinkexist.com/quotation/kindness_in_words_creates_confidence-kindness_in/11355.html (Accessed August 2, 2008).

"Lao-Tzu quotes." Business Coach - Changing Yourself: Starting with Yourself by Vadim Kotelnikov. http://www.1000ventures.com/business_guide/crosscuttings/change_yourself.html (Accessed August 2, 2008).

"Oliver Wendell Holmes quotes." Giga Quotes - John C. Sheppard. http://www.giga-usa.com/quotes/topics/students_t001.htm (Accessed August 2, 2008).

"Kathleen Norris quotes." Common Quotations from Abbe to Zuhav. http://www.phnet.fi/public/mamaa1/quotesnf.htm (Accessed August 2, 2008).

"Eleanor Powell quotes." Brainy Quote. http://www.
brainyquote.com/quotes/authors/e/eleanor_
powell.html (Accessed August 2, 2008).

"Emerald Online Posting." Smile It Cost Nothing.
http://emeralds-diary.blogspot.com/ (Accessed
August 2, 2008).

"Wilson Mizner quotes." QuotationsBook. http://
quotationsbook.com/quote/24030 (Accessed
August 3, 2008).

"Lord Essex quotes." Commercial Solutions Training
and Development. http://commercial-solutions.
com/pages/quotesframeset.html (Accessed August
3, 2008).

"Chinese Proverb quotes." QuotationsBook. http://
quotationsbook.com/quote/41649 (Accessed
August 3, 2008).

"Johann Von Goethe quotes." Wikiquote. http://
en.wikiquote.org/wiki/goethe (Accessed August
3, 2008).

"Dr. Robert Muller quotes." Robert Muller's Good
Morning World #787. http://goodmorningworld.
org/blog/2005/10/gmw-787-establishing-more-
universities.html (Accessed August 3, 2008).

"Laurence Sterne quotes." Wikiquote. http://
wikiquote.org/wiki/Laurence_Sterne (Accessed
August 3, 2008).

"Wilma Askinas quotes". Thinkexist.com. http://
thinkexist.com/quotes/wima_askinas/ (Accessed
August 3, 2008).

"Publius Syrus quotes." QuotationsBook. http://
quotationsbook.com/quotes/36269/ (Accessed 2,
2008).

"Roald Dahl quotes." Brainy Quote. http://www.
brainyquote.com/quotes/r/roaldahl161976.html
(Accessed August 10, 2008).

"Author Unknown." Flying Giants–Rusty Tumble's
blog.   http://www.flyinggiants.com/forums/fg42
/1160-world-models-27-ultimate-bipe-build.
html (Accessed August 12, 2008).

"Ann Landers quotes." Quoteworld.org. http://www.
quoteworld.org/category/laughter/author/ann_
landers (Accessed August 3, 2008).

"Samuel Johnson quotes." Noel's blog. http://
noelkingsley.com/blog/archives/great_quotes/
(Accessed August 3, 2008).

"Author Unknown." The American Enterprise Online.
http://www.taemag.com/issues/articleid.16059
/article-detail.asp (Accessed August 10, 2008).
"Michael Pritchard quotes." The Quotation Page.
http://www.quotationpage.com/quote/23524.
html (Accessed August 3, 2008).

"Chinese Proverb quotes." Holding Headaches at Bay (Body Work Can Ease Chronic Migraines And Tension). http://www.cherokeehealthmassage. com/images/Oct2006.pdf (Accessed August 3, 2008).

"C.S. Lewis quotes." The Quotation Page. http:// www.quotationpage.com/quote/37798.html (Accessed August 3, 2008).

"Voltaire quotes." Brainy Quote. http://www. brainyquote.com/quotes/author/v/voltaire.html (Accessed August 3, 2008).

"Victor Borge quotes." "QuoteDB". http:// wwwquotedb.com/quotes/3139 (Accessed August 3, 2008).

"Wilfred A. Peterson quotes." The Art Of Giving– Mele Cotte blog. http://melecotte.blogspot. com/2007/11/art-of-giving.html (Accessed August 3, 2008).

"Ross Hersey quotes." Quoteworld.org. http://www. quoteworld.org/categories/fera/9/ (Accessed August 3, 2008).

Karl R. Popper. Popper Selections, D. Miller ed., (Princeton, New Jersey: Princeton University Press, 1985).

Jack Birnbaum MD. Cry Anger–A Cure For Depression, (Don Mills, Ontario: General Publishing, 1973).

Irwin Kula with Linda Loewenthal, Yearnings: Embracing the Sacred Messiness Of Life, (New York: Hyperion, 2006).

"Francois Maurac quotes." Quoteworld.org. http://www.quoteworld.org/quotes/8785 (Accessed August 3, 2008).

Gen. Hal M. Hornburg. Air & Space Power Journal–Senior Leader Perspective: What I Believe (March 1, 2005 Ed.). http://www.airpower.maxwell.af.mil/airchronicles/apj/apj05/spr05/hornburg.html (Accessed August 3, 2008).

Walter B. Pitkin. Reflections, The Tribune, Chandigarh, India (June 11, 2004). http://www.tribuneindia.com/2004/20040611/edit.html (Accessed August 3, 2008).

"Patrick Henry quotes." World Of Quotes.com. http://www.worldofquotes.com/topiv/experience/2/index.html (Accessed August 3, 2008).

"Simone Signoret quotes." The Quote Garden. http://www.quotegarden.com/marriage.html (Accessed August 3, 2008).

"Ovid quotes." The Quotation Page. http://www.quotationpage.com/subjects/marriage/ (Accessed August 11, 2008).

"Carl Jung quotes." Wisdom For The Soul by Larry Chang, (Washinton, Gnosophia Publishers, 2006).

"Henry Thoreau quotes." QuotationsBook. http://quotationsbook.com/quote/39995/ (Accessed August 3, 2008).

"Christian Bouvee quotes." Giga Quotes. http://www.giga-usa.com/quotes/topics/honesty_t001.htm (Accessed August 3, 2008).

"Charles Gow quotes." Lightning Success Strategies Inc. http://www.professionalbusinesscoaching.biz/id6.html (Accessed August 3, 2008).

"Rainer Maria Rilke quotes." Marriage Quotes. http://www.wow4u.com/marriage/index.html (Accessed August 3, 2008).

"Confucius quotes." The Quotation Page. http://www.quotationspage.com/quote/24036.htm 1(Accessed August 3, 2008).

"Francois La Rochefoucauld quotes." Romantic Love Quotes. http://www.dindragoste.ro/love/romantic-love-quotes.php (Accessed August 3, 2008).

"John Morley quotes." The Wordsworth Dictionary of Quotations (1998 Edition) by Connie Robertson, (England, Woodsworth Editions, 1998).

"Eleanor Roosevelt quotes." Brainy Quote. http://www.brainyquote.com/quotes/authors/e/eleanor_roosevelt.html (Accessed August 3, 2008).

"Konrad Adenauer quotes." QuotationsBook. http://quotationsbook.com/quote/10801/ (Accessed August 3, 2008).

'Sigmund Freud quotes." Quoteworld.org. http://www.quoteworld.org/quotes/5019 (Accessed August 3, 2008).

"Virgil quotes." Brainy Quote. http://www.brainyquote.com/quotes/authors/v/virgil.html (Accessed August 3, 2008).

"John Locke quotes." The Quote Garden. http://www.quotegarden.com/thinking.html (Accessed August 3, 2008).

"Bertha Von Suttner quotes." Only Love Quotes. http://www.onlylovequotes.com/cute-love-quotes/after-the-verb-to-love-to-help-is-the (Accessed August 3, 2008).

"Carlton Simon quotes." Thinkexist.com. http://thinkexist.com/quote/with/keyword/impulse/ (Accessed August 3, 2008).

"Artemus Ward quotes." World Of Quotes.com. http://www.worldofquotes.com/topic/borrowing/index.html (Accessed August 3, 2008).

"George MacDonald quotes." Xanga posted by Chuckrus. http://www.xanga.com/chuckRus/22764439/item.html (Accessed August 3, 2008).

"Josiah Holland quotes." QuotationsBook. http://quotationsbook.com/quote/34210 (Accessed August 3, 2008).

"John Riskin quotes." Brainy Quote. http://www. brainyquote.com/quotes/authors/j/john_ruskin. html (Accessed August 3, 2008).

"Bernard Baruch quotes." Brainy Quote. http:// wwww.brainyquote.com/quotes/authors/b/ bernard_baruch.html (Accessed August 3, 2008).

"Samuel Coleridge quotes." Brainy Quotes. http:// www.brainyquote.com/quotes/authors/s/ samuel_taylor_coleridge.html (Accessed August 4, 2008).

"Jiddu Krishnamurti quotes." The Wordsworth Dictionary Of Quotes (1998 Edition) by Connie Robertson, (England, Woodsworth Editions, 1998).

"Walter Lippmann quotes." "QuoteDB". http:// www.quotedb.com/quote/3120 (Accessed August 4, 2008).

"Sandra Carey quotes." Quoteworld.org. http://www. quoteworld.org/quotes/2384 (Accessed August 4, 2008).

"Henry Miller quotes." Said What? Quotations. http://www.saidwhat.co.uk/keywordquotes/ surrender (Accessed August 4, 2008).

"Wendell Phillips quotes." The Quotations Page. http://www.quotationspage.com/quote/29056. html (Accessed August 4, 2008).

"Aristotle quotes." Quoteworld.org. http://www.

quoteworld.org/quotes/570 (Accessed August 4, 2008).

"John Wooden quotes." Mazen's Venture Blog, Posted January 17, 2007. http://mazenaraabi.wordpress. com/2007/01/17/its-what-you-learn-after-you- know-it-all-that-counts/ (Accessed August 10, 2008).

"C.W. Ceran quotes." Cybernation.com. http://www. cybernation.com/quotationcenter/quoteshow. php?id=11610 (Accessed August 4, 2008).

"Vincent T. Lombardi quotes." Brainy Quote. http:// www.brainyquote.com/quotes/authors/v/vince_ lombardi.html (Accessed August 4, 2008).

"Elizabeth Bibesco quotes." Thinkexist.com. http:// thinkexist.com/quotation/seeing_through_is_ rarely_seeing/160425.html (Accessed August 4, 2008).

"Donald Laird quotes." Mr. Ikbal Jannif, Address- Graduation Ceremony for the Fiji Institute of Technology, Laucala Bay, Fiji, April 9, 2008.

"Publius Syrus quotes." QuotationsBook. http:// quotationsbook.com/quote/1317/ (Accessed August 4, 2008).

"Swami Sivananda quotes." Welcome to The Quote Garden. http://www.quotegarden.com/effort.html (Accessed August 11 2008).

"Author Unknown." Xanga posted by Cirel. http://

www.xanga.com/cirel/448606890/item.html
(Accessed August 4, 2008).

"Maxim Gorky quotes." Quoteworld.org. http://
quoteworld.org/quotes/5672 (Accessed August 4,
2008).

"Henry Wadsworth Longfellow quotes.".
WorldofQuotes.com.http://www.worldofquotes.
com/topic/Ambition/index.html (Accessed
August 11, 2008)."

"Albert Einstein quotes." Quoteworld.org. http://
www.quoteworld.org/quotes/4168 (Accessed
August 4, 2008).

"Albert Einstein quotes." Quoteworld.org. http://
www.quoteworld.org/quotes/4048 (Accessed
August 4, 2008).

The United Presbyterian Magazine (The Gleaner),
December, 1855, Page 554.

"Nikki Giovanni quotes." Quoteworld.org. http://
www.quoteworld.org/quotes/5453 (Accessed
August 4, 2008).

"Benjamin Disraeli quotes." Quoteworld.org. http://
www.quoteworld.org/quotes/11334 (Accessed
August 4, 2008).

"Hugh White quotes." The Quotations Page. http://
quotationpage.com/subject/mistakes/ (Accessed
August 11, 2008).

"Henry Ford quotes." Quoteworld.org. http://www. quoteworld.org/quotes/10170 (Accessed August 4, 2008).

"Thomas A. Edison quotes." Quoteworld.org. http:// www.quoteworld.org/quotes/b98 (Accessed August 4, 2008).

"Author Unknown." The Road of Life. http://www. cs.cmu.edu/~bsinger/road.html (Accessed August 10, 2008)."Booker T. Washington quotes." Wisdom Quotes: Quotations to inspire and challenge–by Jone Johnson Lewis. http://www.wisdomquotes. com/cat_trust.html (Accessed August 11, 2008).

"Abraham Lincoln quotes." Abraham Lincoln Online–Speeches & Writings. http://showcase. netins.net/web/creative/lincoln/speeches/ cannot.htm (Accessed August 4, 2008).

"J. Lubbock quotes." WorldofQuotes.com, http:// www.worldofquotes.com/author/J-Lubbock/1/ index.html (Accessed August 10, 2008).

"F. Scott Fitzgerald quotes." Thinkexist.com. http:// thinkexist.com/quotation/you_don_t_write_ because_you_want_to_say_something/206031. html (Accessed August 10, 2008).

"Erik H. Erikson quotes." Wisdom Quotes: Quotations to inspire and challenge–by Jone Johnson Lewis. http://www.wisdomquotes.com/ cat_trust.html (Accessed August 11, 2008).

ENDNOTES

1 "Leo Tolstoy quotes," Thinkexist.com, http://thinkexist.com/come/quotes/with/keyword/philosophical/.

2 "Sprichwort quotes," Love Sayings–Joachim Home Page, www.genevieve-cory.isom.com/music/lovesayings.html.

3 "Lao-Tzu quotes," Thinkexist.com, http://thinkexist.com/quotation/kindness_in_words_creates_confidence-kindness_in/11355.html.

4 "Lao-Tzu quotes," Business Coach - Changing Yourself: Starting with Yourself by Vadim Kotelnikov, http://www.1000ventures.com/business_guide/crosscuttings/change_yourself.html.

5 "Oliver Wendell Holmes quotes," Giga Quotes - John C. Sheppard, http://www.giga-usa.com/quotes/topics/students_t001.htm.

6 "Kathleen Norris quotes," Common Quotations from Abbe to Zuhav, http://www.phnet.fi/public/mamaa1/quotesnf.htm.

7 "Eleanor Powell quotes," Brainy Quote, http://www.brainyquote.com/quotes/authors/e/eleanor_powell.html.

8 "Emerald Online Posting," Smile It Cost Nothing, http://emeralds-diary.blogspot.com/.

9 "Wilson Mizner quotes," QuotationsBook, http://quotationsbook.com/quote/24030.

10 "Lord Essex quotes," Commercial Solutions Training and Development/, http://commercial-solutions.com/pages/quotesframeset.html.

11 "Chinese Proverb quotes," QuotationsBook, http://quotationsbook.com/quote/41649.

12 "Johann Von Goethe quotes," Wikiquote, http://en.wikiquote.org/wiki/goethe.

13 "Dr. Robert Muller quotes," Robert Muller's Good Morning World #787, http://goodmorningworld.org/blog/2005/10/gmw-787-establishing-more-universities.html.

14 Ibid

15 Ibid

16 Ibid

17 Ibid

18 Ibid

19 "Laurence Sterne quotes," Wikiquote, http://wikiquote.org/wiki/Laurence_Sterne.

20 "Wilma Askinas quotes," Thinkexist.com, http://thinkexist.com/quotes/wima_askinas/.

21 "Publius Syrus quotes," QuotationsBook, http://quotationbook.com/quotes/36269/.

22 "Roald Dahl quotes." Brainy Quote, http://www. brainyquote.com/quotes/r/roaldahl161976.html.

23 "Author Unknown," Flying Giants–Rusty Tumble's blog, http://www.flyinggiants.com/ forums/fg42/1160-world-models-27-ultimate-bipe-build.html.

24 "Ann Landers quotes," Quoteworld.org, http:// www.quoteworld.org/category/laughter/author/ ann_landers.

25 "Samuel Johnson quotes," Noel's blog, http:// noelkingsley.com/blog/archives/great_quotes/.

26 "Author Unknown," The American Enterprise Online, http://www.taemag.com/issues/ articleid.16059/article-detail.asp.

27 "Michael Pritchard quotes,"The Quotations Page, http://www.quotationspage.com/quote/23524. html.

28 "Chinese Proverb quotes," Holding Headaches at Bay (Body Work Can Ease Chronic Migraines And Tension), http://www.cherokeehealthmassage. com/images/Oct2006.pdf.

29 "C.S. Lewis quotes," The Quotations Page, http: www.quotationspage.com/quote/37798.html.

30 "Voltaire quotes," Brainy Quote, http://www. brainyquote.com/quotes/author/v/voltaire.html.

31 "Victor Borge quotes," "QuoteDB" http://wwwquotedb.com/quotes/3139.

32 "Wilfred A. Peterson quotes," The Art Of Giving–Mele Cotte blog, http://melecotte.blogspot.com/2007/11/art-of-giving.html.

33 "Ross Hersey quotes," Quoteworld.org, http://www.quoteworld.org/categories/fera/9/.

34 Karl R. Popper, Popper Selections, D. Miller ed., (Princeton, New Jersey: Princeton University Press, 1985).

35 Jack Birnbaum MD, Cry Anger–A Cure For Depression, (Don Mills, Ontario: General Publishing, 1973).

36 Ibid

37 Irwin Kula with Linda Loewenthal, Yearnings: Embracing the Sacred Messiness Of Life, (New York: Hyperion, 2006).

38 "Francois Maurac quotes," Quoteworld.org, http://www.quoteworld.org/quotes/8785.

39 Gen. Hal M. Hornburg, Air & Space Power Journal–Senior Leader Perspective: What I Believe (March 1, 2005 Ed.), http://www.airpower.maxwell.af.mil/airchronicles/apj/apj05/spr05/hornburg.html.

40 Walter B. Pitkin, Reflections, The Tribune, Chandigarh, India (June 11, 2004), http://www.tribuneindia.com/2004/20040611/edit.html.

41 "Patrick Henry quotes," World Of Quotes. com, http://www.worldofquotes.com/topiv/ experience/2/index.html.

42 "Simone Signoret quotes," The Quote Garden, http://www.quotegarden.com/marriage.html.

43 "Ovid quotes," The Quotation Page, http://www. quotationpage.com/subjects/marriage/.

44 "Carl Jung quotes," Wisdom For The Soul by Larry Chang, (Washington, Gnosophia Publishers, 2006).

45 "Henry Thoreau quotes," QuotationsBook, http://quotationsbook.com/quote/39995/.

46 "Christian Bouvee quotes," Giga Quotes, http:// www.giga-usa.com/quotes/topics/honesty_t001. htm.

47 "Charles Gow quotes," Lightning Success Strategies Inc., http://www.professionalbusiness coaching.biz/id6.html.

48 "Rainer Maria Rilke quotes," Marriage Quotes, http://www.wow4u.com/marriage/index.html.

49 "Confucius quotes," The Quotations Page, http:// www.quotationspage.com/quote/24036.html.

50 "Francois La Rochefoucauld quotes," Romantic Love Quotes, http://www.dindragoste.ro/love/ romantic-love-quotes.php.

51 "John Morley quotes," The Wordsworth Dictionary

of Quotations (1998 Edition) by Connie Robertson (England, Woodsworth Editions, 1998), Page 296.

52 "Eleanor Roosevelt quotes," Brainy Quote, http://www.brainyquote.com/quotes/authors/e/eleanor_roosevelt.html.

53 "Konrad Adenauer quotes," QuotatiosBook, http://quotationsbook.com/quote/10801/.

54 "Sigmund Freud quotes," Quoteworld.org, http://www.quoteworld.org/quotes/5019.

55 "Virgil quotes," Brainy Quote, http://www.brainyquote.com/quotes/authors/v/virgil.html.

56 "Eleanor Roosevelt quotes," Brainy Quote, http://www.brainyquote.com/quotes/authors/e/eleanor_roosevelt.html.

57 "John Locke quotes," The Quote Garden, http://www.quotegarden.com/thinking.html.

58 "Bertha Von Suttner quotes," Only Love Quotes, http://www.onlylovequotes.com/cute-love-quotes/after-the-verb-to-love-to-help-is-the.

59 "Carlton Simon quotes," Thinkexist.com, http://thinkexist.com/quote/with/keyword/impulse/.

60 "Artemus Ward quotes," World Of Quotes.com, http://www.worldofquotes.com/topic/borrowing/index.html

61 "George MacDonald quotes," Xanga posted by Chuckrus, http://www.xanga.com/chuckRus/22764439/item.html

62 "Josiah Holland quotes," QuotationsBook, http://quotationsbook.com/quote/34210

63 "John Riskin quotes," Brainy Quote, http://www. brainyquote.com/quotes/authors/j/john_ruskin. html

64 "Bernard Baruch quotes," Brainy Quote, http:// wwww.brainyquote.com/quotes/authors/b/ bernard_baruch.html

65 "Samuel Coleridge quotes," Brainy Quotes, http://www.brainyquote.com/quotes/authors/s/ samuel_taylor_coleridge.html.

66 "Jiddu Krishnamurti quotes," The Wordsworth Dictionary Of Quotes (1998 Edition) by Connie Robertson (England, Woodsworth Editions, 1998), Page 215.

67 "Walter Lippmann quotes," "QuoteDB", http:// www.quotedb.com/quote/3120.

68 "Sandra Carey quotes," Quoteworld.org, http:// www.quoteworld.org/quotes/2384.

69 "Henry Miller quotes," Said What? Quotations, http://www.saidwhat.co.uk/keywordquotes/ surrender.

70 "Wendell Phillips quotes," The Quotations Page, http://www.quotationspage.com/quote/29056. html.

71 "Aristotle quotes," Quoteworld.org, http://www.quoteworld.org/quotes/570.

72 "John Wooden quotes," Mazen's Venture Blog, Posted January 17, 2007, http://mazenraabi.wordpress.com/2007/01/17/its-what-you-learn-after-you-know-it-all-that-counts/.

73 "C.W. Ceran quotes," Cybernation.com, http://www.cybernation.com/quotationcenter/quoteshow.php?id=11610.

74 "Vincent T. Lombardi quotes," Brainy Quote, http://www.brainyquote.com/quotes/authors/v/vince_lombardi.html.

75 "Elizabeth Bibesco quotes," Thinkexist.com, http://thinkexist.com/quotation/seeing_through_is_rarely_seeing/160425.html.

76 "Donald Laird quotes," Mr. Ikbal Jannif, Address-Graduation Ceremony for the Fiji Institute of Technology, Laucala Bay, Fiji, April 9, 2008.

77 "Publius Syrus quotes," QuotationsBook, http://quotationsbook.com/quote/1317/.

78 "Swami Sivananda quotes," Welcome to The Quote Garden, http://www.quotegarden.com/effort.html.

79 "Author Unknown" The Best Liberal Quotes Ever by William Martin, http://drwilliampmartin.tripod.com/bigedlist.htm.

80 "Maxim Gorky quotes," Quoteworld.org, http:// quoteworld.org/quotes/5672.

81 "Henry Wadsworth Longfellow quotes," WorldofQuotes.com, http://www.worldof quotes. com/topic/Ambition/index.html.

82 "Albert Einstein quotes," Quoteworld.org, http:// www.quoteworld.org/quotes/4168.

83 "Albert Einstein quotes," Quoteworld.org, http:// www.quoteworld.org/quotes/4048.

84 The United Presbyterian Magazine (The Gleaner), December, 1855, Page 554.

85 "Nikki Giovanni quotes," Quoteworld.org, http://www.quoteworld.org/quotes/5453.

86 "Benjamin Disraeli quotes," Quoteworld.org, http://www.quoteworld.org/quotes/11334.

87 "Hugh White quotes," The Quotations Page, http://quotationpage.com/subject/mistakes/.

88 "Henry Ford quotes," Quoteworld.org, http:// www.quoteworld.org/quotes/10170.

89 "Thomas A. Edison quotes," Quoteworld. org,http://www.quoteworld.org/quotes/b98.

90 "Author Unknown," The Road of Life, http:// www.cs.cmu.edu/~bsinger/road.html.

91 "Booker T. Washington quotes," Wisdom Quotes: Quotations to inspire and challenge–by

Jone Johnson Lewis, http://www.wisdomquotes. com/cat_trust.html.

92 "Abraham Lincoln quotes," Abraham Lincoln Online–Speeches & Writings, http://showcase. netins.net/web/creative/lincoln/speeches/cannot. htm.

93 "J. Lubbock quotes," WorldofQuotes.com, http:// www.worldofquotes.com/author/J-Lubbock/1/ index.html.

94 "F. Scott Fitzgerald quotes,"Thinkexist.com, http:// thinkexist.com/quotation/you_don_t_write_ because_you_want_to_say_something/206031. html.

95 "Erik H. Erikson quotes," Wisdom Quotes: Quotations to inspire and challenge–by Jone Johnson Lewis, http://www.wisdomquotes.com/ cat_trust.html.

listen|imagine|view|experience

AUDIO BOOK DOWNLOAD INCLUDED WITH THIS BOOK!

In your hands you hold a complete digital entertainment package. Besides purchasing the paper version of this book, this book includes a free download of the audio version of this book. Simply use the code listed below when visiting our website. Once downloaded to your computer, you can listen to the book through your computer's speakers, burn it to an audio CD or save the file to your portable music device (such as Apple's popular iPod) and listen on the go!

How to get your free audio book digital download:

1. Visit www.tatepublishing.com and click on the e|LIVE logo on the home page.
2. Enter the following coupon code:
   3c7a-e1d8-f7ca-9c51-e55e-e52b-48b7-796a
3. Download the audio book from your e|LIVE digital locker and begin enjoying your new digital entertainment package today!